THE FORGOTTEN CITIES OF DELHI

Also by Rana Safvi

Where Stones Speak: Historical Trails in Mehrauli, the First City of Delhi

Shahjahanabad: The Living City of Old Delhi

Praise for *The Forgotten Cities of Delhi*

'*The Forgotten Cities of Delhi* takes us to many unknown and remarkable sites within the multiple urban centers of the capital's historic past. On this journey, Rana Safvi recounts vibrant local legends which are in danger of being forgotten. In addition to her stimulating text are many illustrations, especially valuable for locating and understanding the all but forgotten dargahs, tombs, mosques, temples and more.'

– *Catherine Asher, art historian and scholar*

'We owe a profound debt of gratitude to Rana Safvi, whose dedicated research brings alive for us the kaleidoscopic richness of the centuries that are too glibly archived away as "medieval". Safvi is an eloquent and persuasive guide to these pasts – yes, in the plural – whose architectural traces remain with us, yet are in danger of being ignored or erased.'

– *Ranjit Hoskote, poet, art critic, cultural theorist*

'Sharing her own experiences and her favourite poetry, the author invites us to explore not only the forgotten cities and sites of Delhi, but the fascinating stories behind them.'

– *Swapna Liddle, author and historian*

THE FORGOTTEN CITIES OF DELHI

Book Two in the
Where Stones Speak trilogy

RANA SAFVI

Photographs
SYED MOHAMMAD QASIM

HarperCollins *Publishers* India

First published in India in 2018 by
HarperCollins *Publishers* India
4th Floor, Tower A, Building No. 10, Phase II, DLF Cyber City,
Gurugram, Haryana – 122002
www.harpercollins.co.in

4 6 8 10 9 7 5 3

P-ISBN: 978-93-5277-751-8
E-ISBN: 978-93-5277-752-5

Typeset in Adobe Garamond Pro 11.5/16 at
Manipal Digital Systems, Manipal

Printed and bound at
Replika Press Pvt. Ltd.

MIX
Paper from responsible sources
FSC® C016779
FSC www.fsc.org

For Amma and Baba

We are what we are because you brought us up to be ourselves

'to strive, to seek, to find, and not to yield'

CONTENTS

7. HUMAYUN'S TOMB & SURROUNDING AREA 191

8. HAZRAT NIZAMUDDIN BASTI 219

Preface

Maherbaan ho ke bulaa lo mujhe chaaho jis waqt
Main gayaa waqt nahin hun ke phir aa bhi na saku'n
Be kind and call me whenever you please
I'm not time past that I can't come with ease

Mirza Ghalib

Though today a contiguous whole, there used to be many cities within the city of Delhi. If we consider the Tomars as the first dynasty of whom we have documented proof, nine dynasties ruled Delhi till 1857, when it passed on to the hands of the British government and Queen Victoria was crowned the Empress of India in 1876.

These dynasties were:

- Tomar – 10th century–1179
- Chauhan – 1179–1192
- Ghori – 1192–1206
- Slave kings – 1206–1290
- Khilji – 1290–1320
- Tughlaq – 1320–1414
- Saiyyid – 1414–1451
- Lodi – 1451–1526
- Mughal – 1526–1857
- Sur – 1540–1556

Each of these dynasties either built a new capital city or expanded the existing one, giving Delhi a living history of over 1,500 years. There were various reasons for this, the primary one being the need to remain close to sources of water and building in areas with strong defensive positions. The cities therefore kept shifting northward until they culminated in Shahjahanabad.

This book covers the areas between the first city of Mehrauli and the last city of Shahjahanabad. Even today, this is a rich area as far as archaeological diversity is concerned; all kinds of monuments, be they forts, masjids, mandirs, tombs and dargahs, can be found here.

Sultan Alauddin Khilji saw himself as Alexander the Second. He was a highly ambitious ruler with grandiose designs, many of which were left incomplete. The Delhi Sultanate reached its peak under him in terms of administrative prowess, but he couldn't conquer the world like Alexander as he had to contend with insurrections within his kingdom and a very large threat from the Mongols. His ambitious schemes for his kingdom's architecture were left incomplete and he is known for the unfinished Alai Minar and the exquisite Alai Darwaza.

The advent of the Seljuq architects and artisans further fueled the demand for improved architectural skills and capabilities amongst Indian artisans, leading to newer developments in the way kings went about constructing monuments and tombs. For example, Islamic geometrical patterns were woven into local traditions such as the lotus bud motif and the *kalasa*. Most mosques and tombs have the inverted lotus as its crowning glory with a finial on top. The lotus bud has been used as a decorative motif in many doorways from thirteenth-century onwards, with the Alai Darwaza being its best example. This was a major step towards integration of two distinct cultures to become what is now known as Indo-Islamic culture by many historians.

The Tughlaqs constructed three cities under three consecutive rulers. Sultan Firoz Shah was the most prolific of them all. He had the distinction of being the first conservator in India. He not only built new monuments but also repaired and renovated many of the old ones. He built five 'smart' cities too!

The Tughlaq style was very austere, shorn of external ornamentation but built very solidly. Even Quranic calligraphy was missing in their monuments. If there were any paintings, on the walls they have not survived.

Sultan Firoz Shah built many buildings, namely hospitals, madrasas, *shikargahs*, *baolis* and mosques. Seven of Delhi's biggest mosques were constructed during his reign.

The Delhi Sultans built large congregational mosques in the Persian style, with a central open courtyard surrounded by cloistered halls (*iwans*) on three sides with the fourth side being the main prayer hall. These were called four-*iwan* mosques.

Calligraphy was profusely used, as visible in the screens of the Quwwat-ul-Islam mosque or the tomb of Sultan Iltutmish.

Art historian and scholar Catherine Asher says, 'A new theme was introduced in the inscriptions of Iltutmish's tomb, one that became especially important for the Mughals, which is eternal paradise as a reward for the true believer of the Day of Judgement. Thus commenced in India the tradition of paradisiacal imagery for tomb construction. Under the Mughals and culminating with the Taj Mahal, this theme came to be used with extraordinary effect, not only in inscriptions but in the entire conception of the monument.'[1]

Lodi kings were Afghans and in the Afghan tribal system the king was not considered divine or absolute. The nobles felt that too they deserved elaborate funerary buildings and thus in Delhi alone we had more than 100 tombs built under three Lodi kings. The one difference between the royal tombs and the tombs of nobles was not in their size but their shape; the royal tombs were generally octagonal while those of nobles were square in shape.

A unique feature of the Lodi tombs is the extensive calligraphy found on them; however, none of them had their own names inscribed, which today leads to confusion in identifying the name of the person buried. If the names were written on a headstone, locals stole them for use in their own houses.

In fact, the name of Lodi Gardens was originally Bagh e Jadd (garden of the ancestors) and it was a funerary garden for the Lodis. Many accounts say that Sikandar Lodi buried his father, Bahlol Lodi, in Bagh e Jadd. Basheeruddin Ahmad claims his tomb is located in Jodh Bagh; but I feel the name is a corruption of Bagh e Jadd and may have extended all the way to Chiragh Delhi to become today's Jor Bagh, a residential colony.

I've even come across a story stating that Jor Bagh is a corruption of Joru ka Bagh as it was the estate of Nawab Qudsia Begum, the *joru* (wife) of Emperor Muhammad Shah (1719–48 AD). However, Professor Saiyid Zaheer Husain Jafri of the department of history at Delhi University rejects this theory. He says the word 'joru' for 'wife' was not in use in Delhi and no one would disrespect an empress this way. Another tidbit that hints that this theory could be factually incorrect is that most of her constructions, including the dargah at Shah e Mardan (built 1749–51 AD) in present-day Jor Bagh, happened during the reign of her son, Emperor Ahmad Shah Bahadur (r. 1748–54 AD) and not her husband.

The Lodi tombs bear strong resemblance to the Sharqi architecture of Jaunpur and it is possible that the Lodi Sultans brought artists from there after they vanquished the Sharqi kings.

Back then, tombs were part of a flourishing business as many enterprising merchants built tombs for sale and nobles bought them for their burial. That explains some empty tombs found today; they were built but not sold. Locals who inhabited these places in the years that followed stole many of the tombstones for reuse.

The *chaukhat* (door frames) were the favourites for such pilferage as they were usually built using very strong stones and were beautifully built. Gravediggers were also in plenty; they vandalized tombs hoping to find treasure.

The Lodi style of architecture is particularly important because it was the beginning of a unique style which culminated under the Mughals and came to be known as Indo-Persian architecture. The Lodis replaced the large congregational mosques favoured by the Delhi Sultans with single or single-aisled mosques with multiple bays. Lodi architecture was also characterized by the use of coloured stone inlays and blue tiles.

The result of the passage of time on these monuments led to Bishop Heber (1783–1826 AD), who served as the Bishop of Calcutta and travelled all over India, saying in the later part of the nineteenth century that there was in Delhi an 'awful scene of desolation, ruins after ruins, tombs after tombs, fragments of brick-work, freestone, granite, and marble scattered everywhere over a soil naturally rocky and barren, without cultivation, except in one or two small spots, and without a single tree'.[2]

When India's railway lines were being laid, all the monuments that came in the way of its construction were cleared. The most famous target of demolition was the tomb of Princess Zeb-un-Nissa, daughter of Emperor Aurangzeb.

Later, when Lutyens' Delhi was being planned and constructed, a large number of tombs, graves, pavilions, wells and mansions were demolished to make way for new buildings.

Today, modern-day buildings and unorganized settlements have engulfed the remaining ruins, tombs and fragments of history, while many have been eaten up by urbanization.

Since many monuments have been destroyed or forgotten, I have based my book on my own visits, observations and the accounts of two nineteenth-century books which chronicle it, namely Sir Syed Ahmad Khan's (referred to as Sir Syed subsequently) *Asar-us-Sanadid* (1847) and Stephen Carr's *Archaeology and Monumental Remains of Delhi* (1876). Further, Basheeruddin Ahmad's book *Waqiat-e-Darul-Hukumat Dehli* (1919) has powered my narrative with its interesting anecdotes and historical references.

I felt it was important to include their facts and stories as *Asar-us Sanadid* and *Waqiat-e-Darul-Hukumat Dehli* are originally in Urdu and thus can't be read by all.

Maulvi Zafar Hasan's book *Monuments of Delhi: Lasting Splendour of the Great Mughals and Others* (1919) has provided all the architectural information. I am indebted to these four great chroniclers of our heritage for preserving and relaying this precious information to us.

I

Siri

Bastion of Siri Fort

Har shaam yahan, shaam e veera'n aseb zada raste galiya'n
Jis shahr ki dhun mein nikle thay who shahr dil e barbaad kahan?
Every evening is lonely in these haunted lanes
Where is the city in search of which my wounded heart set forth?

Habib Jalib

Skilful masons applied themselves to the work and a new fort was quickly built in place of the old. The new fort with its strong forearm and seven towers shakes hands with the coloured Pleiades, squeezes the powerful Mars under its arm-pit and uses the high sky as a sort of waistband. It is a necessary condition that blood be given to a new building; consequently, many thousand goat-bearded Mughals have been sacrificed for the purpose. When the edifice – many congratulations to its founder – was completed, the Guardian of the Universe took it under His protection. How will any trouble or insurrection find its way to the place of which God is the guardian?[3]

Siri or Dar-ul-Khilafat (seat of the Caliph)

Sultan Alauddin Khilji (1296–1316 AD) built this city between 1297 and 1307 AD to defend his kingdom against Mongol invaders. Initially it was called *lashkar* (military camp) and Mehrauli was *shahr* (city) but later Siri became the *Dar-ul-Khilafat* or Capital City. Its present-day location includes Shahpur Jat, Hauz Khas, Siri Fort and Green Park.

However, the main residence for Sultan Alauddin Khilji apparently remained the *shahr* or Qila Rai Pithaura (Mehrauli). The name 'Siri' was given, according to legend, because some say the heads (*sar* or *sir* in Urdu) of 8,000 defeated Mongols were embedded in the city's foundations. Many believe they are even in the city's walls!

However, Sir Syed quotes *Khulasat-ut-Tawarikh*, an Indo-Persian chronicle by Sujan Rai, that there was a village called Siri on this location and that's why it became famous as Kushk e Siri. At that time it lay between Qila Rai Pithaura and Kilokri, or Naya Shahr.[4]

The fort was circular in shape and its walls were strong, made of lime, stone and bricks. There were seven gates to this fort, as noted by Timur in his memoirs but only the name of the Baghdad Gate is mentioned, which was presumably one of those on the western side. The walls, according to Ibn Batuta, were seventeen feet in thickness but only mounds of earth remain to mark their position. Some parts of Siri's walls can be seen in the Shahpur Jat area. They show a complex double wall with passages in between for the soldiers to move in for defensive purposes and holes for firing arrows.

Siri was the capital of the Delhi Sultans till 1321 AD, after which it was shifted to Tughlaqabad, the city built by Sultan Ghiyasuddin Tughlaq. When Emperor Sher Shah was building his city, Shergarh, much of the material for the building was taken from Siri. Recycling was always in fashion!

Mohammad Wali Masjid

Ghaib ki nazre'n bacha ke kuchh chura le waqt se
Phir na haath aayega kuchh, har lamha hai pa dar rikaab
Steal a few moments from the unknown
Time will slip out of your hands; every moment is ready to ride off

Firaq Gorakhpuri

A gateway leads into an enclosure which contains the mosque. There are a large number of unknown graves in the area next to it.

Mohammad Wali Masjid

This is a three-bay mosque, with a single dome rising from an octagonal drum on the central bay. It is built of dressed hard stone and measures 58 feet × 26 feet. The pendentives inside the dome chamber ornamented with small niches are an interesting architectural feature and look very attractive.

For many years, the villagers there used it as a fodder store. (It was probably cleared in 1924 when ASI got many monuments vacated.) It is a simple mosque but its location in a park full of greenery makes it very scenic. The squinches and medallions with verses from the Quran and Allah's names make it look ethereal.

Tohfewala Gumbad

Aaj zakhmo'n ko mohabbat ki ataa ke badle
Tohfa o tamgha e ahbaab shanaasi likhu'n
Today wounds, gifted in return for love
Seem like a gift for recognizing friends

Farhat Shehzad

This mosque located just inside Shahpur Jat, a heavily congested urban village in Delhi, tantalizes passersby with its majestic dome and high walls as soon as one enters the lane. However, it is not easy to reach it as shops and residential buildings hide its entrance. The spirit of commercialization in Shahpur Jat has overtaken its medieval past.

The Tohfewala Gumbad looks austere and unadorned with a solitary dome reminiscent of the Khilji and Tughlaq era architecture. It is inside an unkempt courtyard with wild grass growing all around but so far no one has encroached inside.

There are niches at the bottom of the dome, on the inside and in the recessed, arched corners. Outside, the dome rests on an octagonal drum decorated with a line of *kanguras*. The mihrab is very simple, consisting of three arched recesses with the central one slightly larger than the ones flanking it. The side opposite the mihrab has three arched entrances while the other two sides have two small arched entrances each and a blocked arched recess in place of the central entrance. A small arched window is provided high in the centre of each side to let in sunlight. There was a staircase on its southern side which led to the top but, as the roof has fallen down, it's no longer accessible. There are ruins of cloisters on the sides, which were probably used as madrasas.

Tohfewala Gumbad

Baradari/Thanewala Gumbad

Ho na kyun vardaat e qatl rozaana abhi
Ku e qatil mein nahin chowki abhi thaana abhi
Who can stop daily bloodshed now?
When there's no police station in the Lover's street now

Shauq Bahraichi

There is confusion about its name as some refer to it as Tohfewala Gumbad and some as Thanewala Gumbad. But, according to Basheeruddin Ahmad, this was actually a ruined *baradari* which was so named as there was a police station near it.

Maulvi Zafar Hasan describes it as 'a rectangular building with a nine-bay central hall, and side chambers to the north and south. Arched openings are visible on the east and west sides and on the north side several vaulted bays are visible.' However, all that remains today is a wall and residential buildings all around it. A local resident in his forties told me that as a child he remembered five families living inside it. As the Shahpur Jat area is now expensive real estate, only a fly can live on that wall; the rest has been gobbled up.

Bulbuliki

Ai aasmaan tere Khuda ka nahin hai khauf
Darte hain ai zameen tere aadmi se ham
O Sky! I don't fear your God
I fear his creations living on land

Josh Malihabadi

Due to prolific construction activity, especially during the Asian Games in Delhi in 1982, quite a lot has already been destroyed. I walked into the Asiad

Bulbuliki

park with a sense of anticipation as I had been told I would find a mosque called Bulbulwaali here.

Luckily I found a helpful gentleman who stays in Shahpur Jat and he guided me. It is behind the Jhankar Banquets (restaurant) and can be accessed from the park side entrance.

When I saw it, it looked like a mosque to me but Zafar Hasan says that it's now a building used as a fodder store by villagers. Whatever it may be, it's in a ruinous condition but looks pretty in its green surroundings. For me, it was of interest as it's from the Khilji period and has survived despite its dilapidated condition.

It has three arched openings in the south and is built of rubble masonry. The roof has now fallen in.

Dargah Makhdoom Sabzwari

Ujaale apni yaado'n ke hamaare saath rahne do
Na jaane kis gali mein zindagi ki shaam ho jaaye
Leave the glow of your memories with me
God knows in which lane the sun may set for me

Bashir Badr

A posh residential colony in Hauz Khas called Mayfair Gardens, though it looks like any other residential area, hides a treasure. Just ahead of the entrance gate is a beautiful Lodi era dargah complex.

The remarkable feature of the gateway of this dargah is the lovely fluted dome on it. The curious might want to venture in and would be greeted by a single-aisle mosque with a big quadrangle. This mosque is locally known as Makhdumki. It is named after a saint, Makhdum Saheb, about whom not much is known.

The notable features, on the west facade of the prayer chamber, are a projected central mihrab, sloping buttresses and a balcony with arched cells. It belongs to the Lodi period (1451–1526 AD). The prayer chamber is internally divided into seven bays, the central one and those on the extreme ends being domed. Quranic ayat are inscribed inside the mosque and the medallions on the facade have 'Allah' inscribed on them.

The mosque itself is in good shape. The doorway to the stairs, which lead to the roof, is locked. It is built of rubble masonry coated with plaster. The mosque forms the western part of an enclosure which contains many graves. There is a single-domed pavilion measuring 17.5 square feet, which is probably for the saint himself. It has twelve columns of local quartzite.

A painting made by Mazhar Khan in the 1840s for Metcalfe's Imperial Delhi shows the presence of beautiful red sandstone lattice screens between these columns, none of which remain today. The inner side of the dome was also beautifully decorated with colourful floral designs. There were inscriptions

Makhdoom Sabzwari Grave and Masjid

of Quranic ayat and some Persian verses on the ceiling but these have since been destroyed. There is a sense of peace here which remains undisturbed by visitors and the occasional scampering squirrel.

From what I gathered via a comment on my blog on the dargah, the descendants had migrated to Pakistan. Metcalfe wrote in his Dehlie Book: 'Durgah ('Shrine') Mukhdoom ('literally a Servant') Subzwaree ('title taken from the place of birth') Saheb. The individual whose shrine is represented here was a native of the town of Subz in the Province of Kish, and was a person of uncommon talent.'[5]

Nili Masjid

Har zarra ubhar ke kah raha hai
Aa dekh idhar! Yahan Khuda hai
Every particle seems to call out
Look this side! God is here

Sufi Tabassum

Nili Masjid

Nili Masjid is located in the village of Kharera, now called Hauz Khas. It is a functioning mosque under Delhi Waqf Board. As per an inscription on its central arch, it was built during the reign of Sultan Sikandar Shah under the governorship of Khan-i-Azam Masnad-i-Ali Khawas Khan by:

'The weak, the infirm and the expectant of compassion from the beneficient God, Kasumbhil, the nurse of the generous and the great Khanzada Miyan Fath Khan, son of Khawas Khan.'

The mosque is built of plastered rubble stone. It has three bays and the central one has a dome on an octagonal drum with small decorative minarets marking the angles. The side bays have flat domes. The east facade is ornamented with a band of blue tiles, which runs above the eave and is surmounted by two incised plaster bands with calligraphy and floral designs. There are minarets flanking the central archway on the top, which are repeated on the eastern corners of the structure too. Conical supporting towers strengthen the back of the mosque. The courtyard of the mosque forms an enclosure with two bastions on either side.

Walls of Siri

Khaamoshi khud apni sada ho aisa bhi ho sakta hai
Sannata hi goonj raha ho aisa bhi ho sakta hai
It could be that the silence is its own voice
It could be that the stillness is echoing in space

Zaka Siddiqui

According to the ASI plaque, only a small portion of the city wall survives in the village of Kharera. A family bought this entire area of the village and the wall is part of their residential property.

Rampant construction activity and urbanization meant the rest of the city walls were demolished to give way to residential buildings. Parts of Siri's walls and ramparts survive in Shahpur Jat village and the 26 acre park near it. A few bastions too have survived. The one that is best preserved is within a small residential area of Shahpur Jat, used as a scooter and cycle stand by locals who are consciously or unconsciously careless and unaware of the historical importance of a thirteenth-century protective city wall. It is the only wall where an inscription can be seen.

The Hauz Khas Gumtis

On the road to the Firoz Shah Madrasa and Tomb complex, there are a number of tombs that are memorials to the aspirations of immortality of unknown men and women.

Dadi Poti ka Gumbad

Dadi Poti ka Gumbad

Yahi hai zindagi kuchh khwaab chand ummeede'n
Inhi'n khilauno'n se tum bhi bahal sako to chalo
This is life, some dreams some hope
Come with me if with just these toys you can cope

Nida Fazli

These are Lodi-era tombs inside Hauz Khas village. The larger one is 52 square feet and is known as Dadi or Biwi ka Gumbad; the smaller one, of 38 feet 10 square inches, is known as Poti or Bandi ka Gumbad. They are both built of rubble masonry with a single dome on top. Both tombs contain unknown graves made of rubble and plaster.

According to local lore, a noble lady had built these tombs; the bigger one being for herself and the smaller one for her *bandi*, a serving lady-cum-friend. However, death has removed all status symbols and both now rest in anonymity.

The dome of Poti's tomb rises from an octagonal drum, crowned by an attractive open hexagonal lantern of red sandstone. On either side of the eastern opening is a staircase leading to the roof but it is out of bounds for tourists.

In the tomb of Dadi the apex of the dome and spandrels of the arches inside are ornamented with painted and incised plaster.

Biran ka Gumbad

Zindagi phaili huyi thi shaam e hijraa'n ki tarah
Kis ko itna hausla tha kaun jee kar dekhta
Life was spread out like an evening of separation
Who had the courage to live through such desolation?

Ahmed Faraz

It is very similar to other Lodi tombs in this area. It stands on a plinth and has a single dome. It measures 42 feet 6 square inches and is constructed of rubble. Inside the tomb is a single grave of an unknown person and it's coated with plaster.

Chhoti Gumti

Band darwaze huye
Barhana vahshat huyi
As the door closes
Stark gloom approaches

Ramesh Kanwal

Chhoti Gumti

This is a domed building in the vicinity of the above-mentioned tomb and is also from the same period. It is built of rubble masonry that's been plastered and measures 15 square inches.

It has arched openings on all four sides and the absence of a mihrab points to the fact that it is certainly not a tomb. However, the purpose of this building is unknown and it is possible it was a doorway to some other building, which has since disappeared, or to one of the many tombs in this area.

Sakri Gumti

Sakri Gumti

Kah ke soya hu'n ye apne iztarab e shauq se
Jab vo aaye'n qabr par fauran jaga dena mujhe
Ere I closed my eyes, I beseeched my restless love
Wake me up as soon as the Beloved comes to my grave

Seemab Akbarabadi

It is a domed structure constructed of rubble masonry, the favourite building material of the Lodi-era, and measures 24 square inches. It has arched entrances on three sides and a mihrab on the west wall. There is a staircase leading to the roof but it's out of bounds for tourists.

Barah Khamba

Andheri qabr mein mujh ko akela chhod jaayenge
Vahan ho fazl se tere ujaala yaa Rasool Allah
I will be left alone in a darkened grave
Let there be light by your grace O Prophet of Allah

Unknown

Any building with twelve columns is called Barah Khamba and, as it was a popular design, you will find references to them in all parts of the country. Since their original name and purpose has been lost, we refer to them as Barah Khamba or Baradari.

This is another Lodi-era structure built of rubble. It is 34 feet 6 inches square with each of its four facades broken by an arch enclosing three arched openings. It stands on a 2 feet 6 inches plinth with a hemispherical dome on top. There were graves inside it that have long disappeared but the compound is full of many other unknown graves.

Eidgah

Ahbaab poochhte hain badi saadagi ke saath
Tuu ab ke saal Eid manaayega kis tarah
Friends ask with great simplicity
How will you celebrate Eid this year?

Unknown

Eidgaah

An Eidgah is different from a mosque as it is used only for the congregational Eid prayers and is an open space which consists of only a mihrab wall and sometimes a minbar or pulpit for the imam to deliver his *khutba*, or message, from.

This Eidgah was made by Iqbal Khan, also known as Mallu Khan, in 1397 when he was in control of Delhi. It measures 190 feet × 173 feet with a 20 feet high wall. The wall is decorated with *kanguras*. There is a thirteen-step staircase next to the central arch that possibly served as a minbar. Built of rubble masonry, this structure has eleven mihrabs and a turret at the end of one side with an inscription. The official inscription gives details of an interesting period of history:

> *In the name of God, who is merciful and clement.*
> *When Qutb-ul-Islam Dar-ul-Hukumat Dehli was desolated by the evil of the accursed Mughal (Mongol) and the mischief of infidels and satans, and had become an abode of wild beasts and birds, and mosques, madrasa, khanqahs, places of worship and charitable foundations were deserted; by the Divine favour and Grace of the Lord, the slave of God named Iqbal Khan also known*

as Mallu Sultani, had the Divine guidance and good fortune, in that he was able by great efforts and endeavours to restore all the charitable foundations and repopulate the capital of Delhi and other parts of the country. He also built this place of worship.

This describes the desolation of Delhi after Timur's invasion. When this Eidgah was built, the ruler, Sultan Nasiruddin Tughlaq Shah had fled to Kannauj and Mallu Khan was in absolute control of Delhi.

Mallu Khan was killed in battle in 1405 against Khizr Khan, the Governor of Dabalpur and Multan.

As a child, I remember going to Eidgahs because there would such a heartwarming atmosphere of camaraderie and happiness after the namaz was over. The highpoint for the children would be the small mela (fair) held just outside the Eidgah where we could buy toys and eatables. This Eidgah is inside Padmini Enclave in Hauz Khas.

Chor Minar

Teg munsif ho jahan daar-o-rasan ho'n shaahid
Begunaah kaun hai us shahr mein qaatil ke siwa
Where the sword is the judge, gallows stand witness
Who else in the city can be innocent except the killer?

Ali Sardar Jafri

In the posh bungalows surrounding Delhi's Hauz Khas area there is a very strange monument which, to me, resembles a lighthouse. The strangeness comes from the fact that Delhi is a landlocked city with no sign of the ocean for miles. However, this monument seems to have a darker side to it.

One has to go into R block of Hauz Khas residential area, where there are two iron gates on the way. Most of the guards in the area will guide you to it as there is no signage there. Only once we go closer to the board do we

Chor Minar

read that it's Chor Minar, built by Sultan Alauddin Khilji (1290–1231 AD) and then used to exhibit the severed heads of thieves during his reign. As per legend, it has 225 holes. The purpose of this minaret was to strike terror in the hearts of people. I can well imagine how terrifying it would be to see 225 severed heads staring at onlookers from that height. Enough to make any sinner turn into a saint! However, no reference is found for this monument in any contemporary text and we can only reach this conclusion based on Sultan Alauddin Khilji's reputation for cruelty and severity. Sultan Alauddin Khilji had come to the throne of Delhi Sultanate at a time when the Mongol threat was escalating and he had to maintain a huge army. He could not, therefore, afford mismanagement, inflation, cheating and deceit, which would have prevented him from facing that threat from a position of strength. This may seem barbaric now but was probably the norm in those times for rulers aiming to run a streamlined administration.

The minar is built of rubble masonry (rough, uncut stones, irregularly set in mortar) and stands in the centre of a platform 30 square feet wide and 7 feet tall. Each of the four sides of the platform has three arched recesses. The central one on the east is a doorway that leads to a spiral staircase. Nowadays there is a grilled gate which is kept locked. If you see it up close, you will smell the stink of pigeons and bats which inhabit it now.

Hauz-i-Alai/Hauz-i-Khas/Hauz e Khas

Att gaye hauz o nahr ghair az chashm
Ek qatra kahin nahin paani
Blocked are the ponds and springs
Not a drop of water in sight

Unknown

This water reservoir, which originally occupied 70 acres of land, was built by Sultan Alauddin Khilji in 1295 AD and was enclosed by a stone and masonry wall. It was repaired by Sultan Firoz Shah in 1354 and refilled with water as it had dried by then. In fact, Sultan Firoz Shah said that people had dug wells in it from which they sold water and used the land for cultivation. He got it cleared, excavated and refilled.

After the repairs and with the establishment of a college on its banks, this reservoir became known as Hauz Khas. Timur wrote in his memoirs that the reservoir was so large that an arrow could not be shot from one side to the other. It was filled by rainwater in the rainy season and the people of Delhi would get water from it all year round. Its area is now severely limited and has become a fashionable and popular social spot with the Deer Park next to it.

Madrasa Sultan Firoz Shah

Jahan se ilm ka hum ko ghuroor hota hai
Vahin se hoti hai bas ibtida jahaalat ki
Where pride enters knowledge
There creeps in ignorance

Azhar Inayati

Madrasa Sultan Firoz Shah

Sultan Firoz Shah built a madrasa on the south and east bank of Hauz Alai in 1352–53 AD. It was a premier institute of its age with the best teachers imparting knowledge in its premises. It provided a very salubrious and picturesque surrounding which was conducive to learning.

The building is made of rubble masonry and dressed stone and originally consisted of a range of double-storeyed buildings extending from the tomb of Sultan Firoz Shah to a distance of 145 feet and 215 feet north and west of the tomb respectively. Though the ruins are extremely magnificent, they are still ruins marked by domes, arches and walls.

There are two well-preserved chambers adjoining the tomb that give an indication of the magnificence of the college. These are double-storeyed and contain arched hallways and windows, projecting towards the reservoir.

There used to be steps leading from the buildings to the Hauz once upon a time, but now although these steps remain, the Hauz has shifted by some distance.

Sir Syed writes that the head of the madrasa was Syed Yusuf bin Jamal Hussaini, who passed away in 1388 AD and is buried in the grounds nearby. Sultan Firoz Shah's tomb is also situated here.

It must have been a truly inspirational place for learning and meditating. There are many pavilions in the compound, which may have been tombs of the teachers. There is a mosque at the extreme north of Firoz Shah's tomb which, according to Basheeruddin Ahmad, was built at the edge of the Hauz. It is a five-arched mosque with two arches on the sides. It is now out of bounds for tourists and the one time I managed to go inside, it was being used as residential quarters for workers who were engaged in repairs of the madrasa.

There were small pavilions built in the wall of the mosque towards the Hauz.

Tomb of Sultan Firoz Shah

Yaad e ayyam ishrat e fani
Na woh hum hain na woh tan asaani
Khaak mein rashk e asmaan se mili
Haaye kaisi buland aiwani
Remembering days of yore is a fleeting pleasure
Neither am I the same, nor the suppleness of body
The envy of the skies turned it into dust
Oh! The lofty mansions and palaces[6]

This *maqbara* (grave) is situated on the side of Hauz Khas. When Sultan Firoz Shah died in 1388 AD he was buried here. According to Sir Syed, this *maqbara* was built during the reign of his son Nasiruddin Muhammad Shah in 1389 AD.

It is built of stone and lime mortar. On its entrance is an inscription in cut-plaster but many of the letters have fallen down; they gave details of its repairs during the reign of Sultan Sikandar Shah.

Tomb of Sultan Firoz Shah

The tomb is a lofty building of 44 feet 6 inches square and is built of stone. Internally it measures 28 feet 7 inches and is paved with grey stone slabs. At the drum level, the square merges into an octagon by deeply recessed arched pendentives and then into a circle for the dome, which is hemispherical. The pendentives are decorated with calligraphy incised on plaster.

The principal entrance is on the south. The door to it is arched and raised on three steps. There is stone latticework on the upper portion of the arch above the lintel.

On the north side is a narrow pointed arch which leads to the madrasa.

The roof was originally richly painted and now has attractive red bands intersecting each other with incised plaster medallions at the point of intersection.

The graves of Nasiruddin Muhammad Shah (son of Sultan Firoz Shah) and Alauddin Sikander Shah (grandson of Sultan Firoz Shah) are also inside the tomb with a fourth unknown grave. Lord Curzon, who was a keen conservationist, did repairs during his time in India. There are many domed pavilions resting on pillars in the compound. Residential buildings overlook the walled enclosure of the madrasa on the southern side.

Bagh e Alam ka Gumbad

Dhundhali si ek yaad kisi qabr ka diya
Aur mere aas-paas chamakta huwa sa kuchh
A faint memory, a flickering lamp on a tomb
And something bright near me

Nida Fazli

This is the tomb of Miyan Sheikh Shihabuddin Taj Khan and was erected by Sultan Abu Saeed during the reign of Sultan Sikandar Lodi in 1501 AD.

This *gumbad* is one of the most attractive Lodi-era tombs and, as it is now inside Deer Park, the flora and fauna around it add to its beauty. It is famous as Bagh-e-Alam, which indicates that there may have been a garden

Ceiling of Bagh e Alam ka Gumbad

around it, so the present location does it justice. It is built of dressed stone while the dome, which covers it, is made of rubble masonry with plaster on top.

There are archways with a doorway on three sides, with a qibla mihrab wall on the western wall. The red sandstone mihrab is decorated with Quranic inscriptions. There is a cusped arch and pendent on the centre.

The main entrance on the south has a red sandstone architrave ornamented with blue tiles. There are three small niches of red sandstone with a small balcony on the arched opening.

There are two staircases on the eastern walls with steps leading to the roof. I climbed up to the dome to find modern-day graffiti painted on it as well as broken beer bottles.

The dome springs from a sixteen-sided drum and that is, along with the parapet, edged with *kanguras*. There are several unknown graves inside the tomb, which measures 33 feet 10 inches square. The wall mosque next to it has five mihrabs pointing to Mecca with pretty octagonal towers flanking it on either side. A pretty picture, but it is now full of graves and is more a cemetery than a mosque.

Kali Gumti

Zindagi yu'n huyi basar tanha
Qaafila saath aur safar tanha
Life went past as if
All alone in the crowd

Gulzar

It's a small tomb measuring 17 feet 6 inches square with a wall mosque attached to it. It stands very close to Bagh-e-Alam ka Gumbad. This tomb is very nondescript and it's the surroundings which make it attractive.

This *gumti* also lies inside Deer Park in Hauz Khas Village.

Kali Gumti

Tuhfewala Gumbad

Na ibtida ki khabar hai na intiha maaloom
Raha ye wahm ki ham hain so vo bhi kya maaloom
Where will life start where will it end, we know not
As for the illusion that we exist, that too we know not

Fani Badayuni

A little walk amongst the greenery of Deer Park leads one to this *gumbad*. It's on a high platform and difficult to reach unless one knows where to go. I was helped by one of the guards in locating it. It is made of rubble masonry and measures 32 square feet. It has been plastered on top. There are many unknown graves inside it that are probably it Lodi nobles. It has four doorways and I feel that the western door must have been closed with rubble masonry walls at some point as all tombs normally have a mihrab wall.

I visited it soon after Holi and there was colour on the graves. It's a custom of the locals to go and offer colour at the mazars as they consider them pirs (patron saints).

Dargah Bibi Zuleikha (Mai Saheba)

I am a traveler, You are my road.
I go from You to You.

Zeynep Hatun[7]

Her Holiness Bibi Zuleikha Saheba, the venerable mother of his holiness Sultan-ul-Mashaikh (chief of the saints), Mehboob e Ilahi Sheikh Nizamuddin Auliya, may God purify their graves, repaired to the next world on the first of Jumada II in the year 648 Hijra (31 August 1250 AD).

Dargah Bibi Zuleikha (Mai Sahiba)

This inscription is on the northern wall of the grave chamber of Bibi Zuleikha, also known as Mai Saheba. She was buried in the same room where she lived. Like many other families of central Asia, Bibi Zuleikha's parents Khwaja Ali and Khwaja Arab migrated to India during the Mongol invasions of Bukhara. They settled down in Badayun, then an important town in Awadh (now Uttar Pradesh). Khwaja Arab gave Bibi Zulekha in marriage to Khwaja Syed Ahmad.

There are many legends associated with her. The most famous one was that she chose her son over her husband when she was asked to make a choice between them in a dream as only one was destined to live. Her husband passed away soon after and left Bibi Zuleikha feeling remorseful. She was only comforted by the fact that she had no control over her dreams as these are involuntary experiences and life and death are a matter of God's will.

Mai Saheba was a devoted mother and ensured her children received the best of everything despite severe hardships in her life. She ensured that her son was educated under the care of the best scholars of Badayun and once she felt her son had outgrown them, the family shifted to Delhi so that he could pursue his education. Hazrat Nizamuddin Auliya was sixteen then.

Whenever there was no food in the house, Mai Saheba would tell her son, 'Nizam! Today we are the guests of Allah.' She had total belief in God's will and taught her children that He would send spiritual nourishment that differed from worldly food.

Hazrat Nizamuddin Auliya wrote that when his mother prayed, she appeared to be in direct communication with God. He would witness her prayers being accepted without any delay. Every month, on sighting the new moon, he sought the blessings of Mai Saheba, placing his head on her feet. He wrote that just before she left the world, she was ill for a few days and would often weep.

On the night of the new moon when he presented himself before her and kissed her feet, she asked her son tearfully, 'Nizam! Whom will you go to on the next new moon night and who will look at you with as loving a gaze as mine?'

When her weeping and distressed son asked her, 'O Maqdooma e Jahan, in whose care will you entrust me?' she told him to go and sleep in the adjoining house of Sheikh Najibuddin Mutawakkil and said she would tell him the next day. He spent the night in anguish and as soon as dawn broke, rushed to her side and fell crying at her feet. She held her son's right hand and whispered, 'O Allah, I entrust my son to Thy care,' and recited the *kalima* before leaving this world for the next.[8] Hazrat Nizamuddin Auliya said that he felt a deep state of contentment after those words.

The entrance to Mai Saheba ki Dargah is through a narrow lane in Adchini. Once upon a time it had its own doorway with a *baoli* inside it. Today, it is a very well maintained dargah, most of which has been renovated and built recently. There is a beautiful chandelier in the shrine chamber that has a glass decoration on the roof, giving it a beautiful hue. There are other graves in the chamber and her daughter Bibi Jannat's grave is by her side. The other graves include Bibi Zainab, the daughter of Bibi Jannat.

The graves of Bibi Hoor and Bibi Noor, daughters of Sheikh Shahabuddin Suhrawardi, are also inside the mosque. The house belonged to Sheikh Shahabuddin Suhrawardi. In fact, the locals called the area Bibi Noor ki Basti during the twentieth century.

It is one of the few Delhi dargahs where women can go inside and pray for as long as they want. It is said that Mai Saheba can't bear to see anyone sad and helps in fulfillment of wishes. I go there often to sit and meditate and gain peace of mind. My only complaint is against the caretakers of the dargah who often ask for donations. It is completely against the spirit of a lady who never asked for anything from anyone except Allah.

There is a new mosque in place of the old one. A *langarkhana* provides rice and dal to everyone who comes there.

The locals told me that the word Adchini comes from *Adh-chuni*, half plastered, and till date every building in this area is plastered only partially.

Dargah Sheikh Najibuddin Mutawakkil

Do not follow a truth, which resembles lie.

Baba Farid Ganj e Shakkar

Behind Mai Saheb's dargah, a little distance away is the Dargah of Sheikh Najibuddin Mutawakkil, the brother and *khalifa* of Baba Farid Ganj e Shakkar and teacher of Hazrat Nizamuddin Auliya. It is a simple dargah with one room containing two graves in the centre and two small ones on the sides. It is in a small compound next to a brand new mosque.

The first grave is of Bibi Fatima Saheba, daughter of Baba Farid Ganj e Shakkar. The other two are of the infant sons of Sheikh Najibuddin Mutawakkil: Sheikh Ahmed and Sheikh Ismail.

Sheikh Najibuddin was a scholar saint of great repute. His grave at the back of the enclosure says that he died in 671 AH (1272–73 AD) but, according to Basheeruddin Ahmad, this date is wrong and he had passed away in 1280 AD.

He lived in Delhi for seventy years and seemed to have had no known means of livelihood; the title 'mutawakkil' comes from that as it means 'he who is resigned to the will of Allah'. Sheikh Najibuddin was totally unconcerned with the world to the extent that he wouldn't know what date or month it was. He did not even recognize the currencies or coins which were presented to him as tribute.

A special function used to be held in his house on Eid, called 'Dervesho'n ki Eid', when mendicants from all over the city would gather. One day it so happened that he didn't have any money to feed the gathering. He immediately went up to the roof of his house and started praying to Allah. For once he felt some apprehension in his heart over how he would feed everyone.

Soon he saw an old gentleman come to the roof who said:

Dargah Sheikh Najibuddin Mutawakkil

Ba dil guftam dila Khizr ra beeni
Dil guft agar mara numayid beenam
I asked my heart would you like to see Khizr?
My heart cried out, why not if you show him to me

The old gentleman put some food in front of him and said, 'Your *tawakkul* [trust in God] is being praised in the heavens and you are in such a state!'

Sheikh Najibuddin replied, 'Allah knows the truth. I have never asked for anything for myself. This fleeting apprehension was only because of the people gathered in my house.' According to legend, the old gentleman was Hazrat Khwaja Khizr.[9]

Another famous incident is about Hazrat Nizamuddin Auliya, who came to meet Sheikh Najibuddin before he became a disciple of Baba Farid Ganj e Shakkar.

Sheikh Najibuddin and Hazrat Nizamuddin Auliya lived in adjoining houses close to this shrine. He asked Sheikh Najibuddin to pray that he could become a Qazi. Sheikh Najibuddin remained silent. When Hazrat Nizamuddin Auliya came a second time with the same request he replied, 'Why do you want to become a Qazi? You are destined for something else.'

II
Tughlaqabad

Tughlaqabad Fort (Courtesy: ASI archives)

Gum hain tanhaiyo'n mein shahr ka shahr
Kaise in jangalo'n ko paar kare'n?
Entire cities are lost in loneliness
How can one cross these jungles?

Shabnam Rumani

Sultan Ghiyasuddin Tughlaq (1321–1325 AD) started construction of this city in 1321 AD. The construction must have happened at a fairly quick pace; Sir Syed says it was completed in two years. It seems like a remarkable feat given its size and solidity.

Basheeruddin Ahmad, when describing his journey to Tughlaqabad in the early twentieth century, said that the rocky, hilly road from Mehrauli to Tughlaqabad was so bad that he preferred to walk rather than getting his bones jolted in a bullock cart. He even describes an interesting monument on the way of which no trace remains. On this road, towards the left, was a monument called Sau Baato'n ka Gumbad. It was an octagonal *baradari* and it is said that it contains the grave of a fakir who had conversed a hundred times with Allah. It was a lofty walled enclosure and though it no longer remains, I found the story very fascinating.

Tughlaqabad Fort

Waqt se pooch waqt se sachha shaahid koi nahin
Kis ne tegh uthayi rann mein, kis ne sipar daali
Ask time, there is no truer witness than Time
Who fought the good fight and who surrendered?

Mohammad Ahmad Ramz

Tughlaqabad Fort

There is a very interesting story behind the construction and desolation of this fort. The proverb 'Man proposes and God disposes' is probably true.

Ghazi Malik, the much celebrated and undefeated general of the Khilji Sultanate, was the son of a Turk father and a Hindu Jat woman. By dint of his ability, Malik rose to the position of a provincial governor.

After the death of Sultan Alauddin Khilji, the Sultanate was in turmoil. Sultan Qutb-ud-din Mubarak Shah (ruled 1316–20 AD) succeeded Sultan Alauddin Khilji, his father. However, Khusro Khan removed him within a year and ruled as Sultan Nasiruddin Khusro Shah for a short period of time. He turned out to be a very unpopular Sultan.

Ghazi Malik stepped into that breach and was crowned the Sultan, becoming the founder of the Tughlaq dynasty. Once he accompanied Sultan Alauddin Khilji's son, Sultan Qutb-ud-din Mubarak Shah, to the area where this fort is located. Impressed by its natural defensive position he mentioned that it would be an ideal place for a fort, to which the Sultan replied he could make it into one if he ever became Sultan! So one of his first acts was to start construction of this fort.

The story of its destruction is the stuff legends are made of. Hazrat Nizamuddin Auliya, the popular Sufi saint, was a contemporary of Sultan Ghiyasuddin Tughlaq. One of the principles of the saint was to spend his time in prayers, devotion to God and service to mankind. He stayed away from the courts of the sultans.

His *khanqah* was a refuge for the poor and rich alike, and he did not differentiate between them. His kitchens fed thousands daily, irrespective of caste, creed or status. When Khusro Khan became the Sultan he is believed to have given five lakh rupees to the saint, probably to win him over to his cause. The saint took it and as was his custom, before the sun had set, he distributed it amongst the poor and needy people. When Sultan Ghiyasuddin Tughlaq came to the throne, he declared all grants and titles given by the previous Sultan as illegal and demanded them back.

Hazrat Nizamuddin Auliya had already distributed it and said that he had not used it for himself so could not return it. Sultan Ghiyasuddin Tughlaq was unhappy on hearing this. Thus started a series of episodes that showed the growing feud between the practical, rough and ready Sultan and the popular, generous and reclusive saint.

Hazrat Nizamuddin Auliya was building a *baoli* in his *khanqah* for the use of his devotees who came from far and wide. The fort of Tughlaqabad was also being built at the same time and the Sultan had ordered that all resources be directed there. There rose a conflict of interest as labourers preferred to work for the saint. The Sultan decreed that all labourers had to work on his fort or be ready for dire consequences.

The labourers who also were his devotees started working at the saint's *baoli* at night. Not to be outdone, the Sultan forbade the sale of oil in order to prevent them from working in the dark. However, according to legend, with the blessings of the saint, his disciple Hazrat Roshan Chiragh e Dilli performed a miracle wherein water filled in the lamps became oil.

Hazrat Nizamuddin Auliya is said to have cursed the Sultan's Fort:

Ya rahe ujar,
yaa basse gujjar
May it remain desolate and unoccupied
Or inhabited only by herdsmen

Syed Farid Nizami, the *naib sajjada nasheen* of Dargah Hazrat Nizamuddin Auliya and his direct descendant, related another interesting story to me.

Once Hazrat Nizamuddin Auliya was called to the court of Sultan Ghiyasuddin Tughlaq in Tughlaqabad; in fact, this was the only time he went to the court of a king. This was to attend a meeting on the practice of listening to music in *sema mehfils*. Various saints, scholars and noblemen were invited for the discussion.

When the saint appeared, the entire assembly of nobles gathered there stood up to pay their respects to him. This didn't go down well with the Qazi-ul Sultan, the Chief Justice who was presiding over it as though he thought he was the main hero of that room as the convener of the assembly. He showed his pen to the saint and said, 'I can write your fate with it.' Hazrat smiled and said, 'You could be dismissed before you do that!'

The saint presented a Hadith of the Prophet (Sahih al Bukhari no. 907) where the Prophet (pbuh) had permitted Ayesha to listen to singing and instruments, once at a wedding and once on the occasion of Eid. In fact, as Imam al Ghazali said, 'The Prophet prevented Abu Bakr and Umar from interrupting and scolding the players and singers, telling Abu Bakr that this festival was a joyous occasion and that singing was a means of enjoyment.'[10]

The Qazi was annoyed at having his argument proved wrong as he had wanted music banned. He got up and asked that he be given some evidence that Imam Hanafi had sanctioned music, as they were both his followers. Imam Hanafi was the founder of the Sunni Hanafi school of fiqh (jurisprudence). Hazrat Nizamuddin Auliya got up, saying that he didn't want to participate in such an assembly where the Prophet's Hadith was not accepted as final proof.

According to Syed Farid Nizami it is then that he cursed the court and fort and said that a court where the Hadith of the Prophet is not accepted and imams are given more importance would never prosper. He prophesied its desolation:

Ya rahe ujar,
yaa basse gujjar

This fort was part of the *jageer* of Raja Nahar of Ballabhgarh. The British confiscated it as the Raja sided with Emperor Bahadur Shah Zafar in the first war of Indian independence of 1857.

The fort is an irregular half-hexagon and stands on a scarped outcrop of rock. The imposing fort walls are visible for miles around and bear testimony to the art of their builders. There used to be a moat running around it.

The walls are built of massive blocks of stone of extraordinary thickness which were quarried on the spot. According to Carr Stephens, one stone weighed by General Cunningham measured 14 feet × 2.5 feet × 2.2 inches × 1 feet 10 inches and weighed more than six tons.[11] You can imagine the effort that went into building the wall alone; perhaps that is why it survived and wasn't stripped to build another subsequent city.

The wall on the southern side is 40 feet high with loopholes for the soldiers to shoot arrows from. A line of *kanguras* measuring 7 feet crowned these. Since the terrain is sloping in the places where it dips, the height of the wall goes up to 90 feet to even it out on the top.

We enter the fort by a small postern gate at the head of a winding approach. One cannot be prepared for the wilderness and undergrowth that meets us when we step inside the premises. Hazrat Nizamuddin Auliya's prophecy seems to have come true as I even found cattle tied here!

Sir Syed writes that in the middle of the fort there used to be a lofty building that was the Sultan's Baithak, named Jahannuma, or 'like the Universe'. He also adds that this city and fort had fifty-six *kot* and fifty-two gates. Many of the bastions still guard the fort and some of the gates are set in them but it's impossible to count how many remain. General Cunningham has talked of only thirteen gates, some of which are:

- The Delhi Darwaza, the Neemwala Darwaza, the Dhoban Darwaza to the west.
- The Chaklakhana Darwaza to the north.
- The Bhati Darwaza, the Rawal Darwaza and the Bindaoli Darwaza to the east.
- The Andheri Darwaza and Hathi Darwaza to the south.
- Some other gates were called Khirki Darwaza, Khujoorwala Darwaza, Chowk Darwaza, Hodi Darwaza, Lal Ghanti Darwaza, Tehkhana Darwaza and Talaqi Darwaza.

We can see some of these gates more clearly from Adilabad Fort. We can see ruined buildings all over the fort with underground passages in a line with the central gateway, which may have once been stables or rooms for retainers. Though the leopard or the skulking jackal mentioned by G.R. Hearn is no longer there, it is still not advisable for people to go in there alone. The two-legged animals who sometimes lurk there are worse.

Now we see only ruins, but Joseph David Beglar had attempted to resurrect the plans of the buildings inside. He says that there was a third smaller enclosure in the citadel; the space within this enclosure is full of ruins of small houses, apparently dwelling houses, in all probability or the king's *zenana* (private residence) and domestic offices. The houses are all small without a single window.[12]

The general plan included courtyards with buildings on three sides and sometimes on all four. There was only one entrance set in the enclosure wall to these buildings. In front of the gate of most of these courtyards was a hall measuring 22 feet × 12 feet with two rooms on either side which opened to the courtyards. Sometimes the halls had a range of small rooms at the back. Every room had innumerable arches but no windows which opened outside.

Beglar goes on to say: 'It is difficult to imagine that the king lived in such a miserable place but that appears to have been the fact.'

There must have been grand palaces, mosques, etc., but those were for public and not for personal use. There were underground apartments in the fort, 30 feet to 80 feet deep on a level with large wells or tanks faced with stone. The royal apartments were a suite of eight circular rooms with arched roofs and a space of 2 feet in diameter at the top for ventilation. These rooms were used in the summers, though they don't appear to have been used.

On either side of the gateway are more magnificent ruins. A row of arches standing alone is eye-catching. The tallest bastion inside the fort was known as Sher Mandal, according to Basheeruddin Ahmad, and was ideally placed not just to see the whole fort but the entire city. When it was built, Sultan Ghiyasuddin's eye must have often fallen on the Qutub Minar, away to the west.

Near Sher Mandal is an impressive *baoli* that measures 111 feet × 77 feet and is 70 feet deep. It can be reached by a flight of stairs and, even in its desolation, it speaks of its aspirations of providing water to a city that should have flourished but didn't. One of the reasons given for this is that the water was brackish.

The ruins on the side of the *baoli* seem to have been the palace. There is even a structure with a sunken tank and pipes, possibly a hammam (public bath chamber). There used to be a lake to the rear of the Qila that provided water for the army, but it is no longer extant.

There are rooms near this *baoli* which were royal residential quarters. A long tunnel also existed here, albeit in a ruined condition, till the twentieth century. It led outside the fort and had windows for ventilation and light but now there are no traces of it. There were seven lakes and three *baolis* in Tughlaqabad but today only two *baolis* can be seen. There were ruins of a Birij Mandir and

Jama Masjid in the city which no longer exist. These massive cyclopean walls still stand despite the ravages of time and the workmen who built such strong walls deserve our salute. Though the buildings inside have collapsed, the walls still guard the fort and they still attract hundreds of visitors.

Zameen e chaman gul khilati hai kya kya
Badalta hai rang aasmaan kaisa kaisa!
The soil of the garden gives birth to such bloom
The sky changes colours from boom to doom

Haider Ali Atish

Tomb of Sultan Ghiyasuddin Tughlaq Shah

Jaam uthha aur dil ko zinda rakh
Aasmaan maqbara hai sadiyo'n ka
Lift your cup and drink to Life
The sky is a mausoleum of the ages

Abdul Hamid Adam

Ghiyasuddin Tughlaq, the courageous Sultan who defeated the Mongols so convincingly that they didn't look towards Hindustan for as long as he ruled, died not in the battlefield but during a reception to felicitate his victory.

After a victorious campaign in Bengal, the Sultan stopped at Afghanpur, six miles away from Delhi. His heir, Prince Junan Khan (Muhammad bin Tughlaq), erected a wooden palace for his reception in a record three days under the supervision of a certain Ahmed ibn Ayaz, who was later rewarded with the title of Khwaja Jahan.

This canopy collapsed over the Sultan after the reception and crushed him to death. There are two versions for the collapse: Ziauddin Barani said it was due to lightning and Ibn Battuta said it was built to collapse if an elephant pushed it.

Tomb of Sultan Ghiyasuddin Tughlaq Shah

It is said that Prince Junan Khan took permission to parade his elephants and asked his friends to leave the tent.

The Sultan's favourite son, Mahmud, was also with him. The tent fell down as soon as the elephants passed by it and the prince prevented timely help from reaching the father. Although this mishap took place in the afternoon, it was only in the evening that the canopy was removed from top. It is said that the Sultan had his arms wrapped around Mahmud as if to protect him.

Sultan Ghiyasuddin Tughlaq did not approve of the closeness between Junan Khan (who ascended the throne as Sultan Mohammad bin Tughlaq) and Hazrat Nizamuddin Auliya, given their troubled history. This, combined with the saint's curse, led Sultan Ghiyasuddin Tughlaq, who was on a campaign in Bengal, to ask the saint to leave Delhi before his return or face dire consequences. His followers were worried when they heard of the Sultan's approach and imminent entry in Delhi. They advised him to leave Delhi and shift to Multan but an unperturbed Hazrat Nizamuddin Auliya, who placed his trust in Allah, just said simply:

Hunuz Dilli dur ast
Yet, Delhi is far away

Now it is a matter of conjecture and faith if you want to believe that there was a conspiracy to kill the Sultan and that Hazrat Nizamuddin Auliya was a party to it because Muhammad bin Tughlaq was his follower or to repose your faith in the man of God who had total trust in Him and so refused to relocate.

Professor Mohammad Habib writes that this story is a latter-day fabrication as neither Ziauddin Barani nor Amir Khurd, the two historians of his age, mention anything concerning the 'unpleasantness between the two old men, who were so eminently virtuous in their different spheres of life'.[13]

Junan Khan was devoted to the saint and was one of the people who carried his funeral bier. In a state of divine ecstasy (*wajd*), Hazrat Nizamuddin Auliya had predicted that he would wear the crown.

Abul Fazl has refuted Ibn Battuta and said that, since the canopy had been built hurriedly, it was not strong enough to withstand the circumstances and there was no intent to kill on the part of Prince Junan Khan.

The Sultan was buried in the tomb he had built for himself earlier. This incident took place in February 1325 AD.

The tomb lies opposite the Tughlaqabad Fort and was known as Dar-ul-Aman or 'abode of peace'. Apart from its beauty, it assumes architectural importance as it is one of the first monuments to combine a red sandstone body and a white marble dome as well as the lotus *kalasa* on top.

Sultan Ghiyasuddin Tughlaq had already built a very beautiful tomb for himself in Multan when he was governor of Dipalpur. It was called Rukn e Alam, named after Sheikh Ruknuddin, a Suhrawardi saint whom he revered. It is said that Sultan Muhammad bin Tughlaq presented the tomb to the saint in an attempt to gain his goodwill.

Sultan Ghiyasuddin Tughlaq built another one in Delhi for himself and as a concession to the times he lived in, it was heavily fortified with four strong bastions. It was named Dar-ul-Aman, perhaps following the tradition of the name of Sultan Balban's tomb in Mehrauli.

The fortified enclosure is an irregular pentagon, probably to fit into the shape of the rocks it was built on. Its irregular shape also gave rise to another name: Tikonia Kot or Triangular Fort. A fit resting place for a warrior king!

The fortification and its situation in a lake also made it possible to use this little fort as a summerhouse. The approach used to be by a 27-arched causeway on the lake. Today there is no trace of the lake but part of the causeway still exists; though a portion of it was demolished to make way for the Mehrauli-Badarpur Road.

The entrance to the enclosure is a lofty gateway with a bastion closeby, built to prevent forceful entry as there is a sharp turn and the steps are open to attack from above.

As in the fort, here too the masonry is magnificent with massive stones, many of which must weigh five tons apiece. The red sloping walls with battlements and the gateway together combine to give an effect of stern grandeur. It's a monument which can be seen from afar and it has never failed to thrill me as a fine example of medieval architecture.

Hearns writes that the parapet is raised and the embrasures (slits in the walls for firing) are rather curious: three upright stones forming two openings for fire with a curved stone across the top to protect the head. He points to another feature in the surrounding walls to be noticed: Hindu pillars, lintels, and slabs are introduced in places and break the monotony of the arcades below the parapet.

The interior of the fortified enclosure is raised and is probably built above an outcrop of rock; or this may have been arranged to provide the height for the underground apartments. There are four red sandstone *dalans* (galleries) inside the enclosure that were intended to function as a madrasa. This was a regular medieval custom as it provided students, who would not only sanctify the area with religious studies but could also pray regularly for the departed souls. Under the Tughlaqs, the mendicants used this and later the villagers habituated it.

Hearn writes: 'In the arcade to the left of the entrance there is a small grave, which is reputed to contain the bones of the favourite dog of Tughlak Shah; this is a wonderful tribute to that animal, when we remember that dogs are considered unclean by Mahomedans.'

Basheeruddin Ahmad also writes that there is a popular belief that it is the tomb of a dog, with a quartzite headstone measuring 2.5 feet × 1.3 feet and 1.7 feet in height, but he doubts it. He says that it is a tombstone from some man's grave that has been ensconced in this arcade. Since Muslims consider the dog an unclean animal, there is no possibility of making a tomb for it, he says, adding further that it is a false story spread by people. I have not seen this tombstone myself nor is there any reference to it in modern descriptions.

The only grave chamber that I have seen is to the right of the gate and has been listed by ASI as that of Zafar Khan. The inscription put by Archaeological Society of India on the southern side says: 'This tomb houses the remains of Zafar Khan, who was a general of Sultan Alauddin Khilji.'

The inscription over Zafar Khan's tomb states that it was built by Majlis e Aala (Sultan Ghiyasuddin Tughlaq) for the deceased Khan. The inscription also describes him as having been a conqueror of many lands but who (curiously) died as a mere child! There are two graves inside the tomb, one of which is that of a child. It is octagonal and measures 19.5 feet in diameter and is very pretty. The dome rests on eight pillars with two openings and that results in it being dark inside. There is profuse calligraphy on the tomb.

It seems that Sultan Ghiyasuddin Tughlaq built Dar-ul-Aman for this unknown Khan and during its construction he may have realized it was an ideal place for his own tomb. That may be the reason why Zafar Khan's tomb is built in the walls while his is in the centre.

The tomb has a marble dome which rises above the walls in the centre of the fortified enclosure and measures 26 feet 3 square inches and 70 feet in height, with sloping walls of red sandstone crowned with battlements. The western wall has a *qiblagaah* and the three other sides have doorways superimposed with small arched openings filled with marble lattice screens. The edge of the main gateway arch on all four sides is trimmed with lotus buds, which were first introduced in Alai Darwaza.

The walls and gateways use marble for trimming and edging. The *qiblagaah* is white marble with black marble bands on top.

The dome rises from an octagonal drum and, as mentioned above, is surmounted by a red sandstone finial with a lotus base. Strangely, there is no staircase to the top.

There are three graves inside – Sultan Ghiyasuddin Tughlaq, his wife Makhdoom e Jahan, his son and his successor son Sultan Muhammad bin Tughlaq.

Sir Syed, in his first edition of *Asar-us-Sanadid,* says that he does not know who the person buried in the third grave is as Sultan Ghiyasuddin Tughlaq had no son named Mohammad Adil Shah – which was the name it was known by. It seems that the viciousness, sharp mood swings and temperament of the genius but eccentric Sultan Muhammad bin Tughlaq led to his name falling into disuse. An unjust king could not be remembered by a just name, the literal meaning of Adil.

Ibn Battuta writes that he had not seen a more generous man than Sultan Muhammad bin Tughlaq or a crueler one. On one hand, he would donate to charity so generously as if there was no tomorrow and on the other, rivers of blood would flow on his orders.

His successor, the more balanced and pious Sultan Firoz Shah, not only had a sandal canopy built over these graves and curtains from the sacred Kaa'ba in Mecca put over it, he also searched for and got letters of forgiveness from those people and their heirs who had been tortured, maimed, killed or persecuted by Sultan Mohammad Adil Tughlaq Shah. He got these letters sealed inside a box and kept it near the head of the grave.

I wonder if it worked or it was just humans fooling themselves!

It is said there are two types of rights as per Islam: one is *Huq-ul-Allah* (Duties towards God and Rights) and the other is *Huquq-ul-abad* (Duties towards mankind and rights). There is a Hadith of the Prophet that on the Day of Reckoning, God will forgive those sins and injustices committed against persons only if that person forgives first. It was in this belief that Sultan Firoz Shah sought for forgiveness for his predecessor.

Mumkin nahin abd se ibadat teri
Lutf o karam o ata hai aadat teri
Qatra qatra hain go ke asiyaa'n mere
Dariya dariya magar hai rahmat teri
It's impossible for the devotee to worship You
Granting rewards, giving gifts is Your Habit
Even if miniscule are my sins
Like the ocean is Your mercy

Unknown

Near this *maqbara*, Sultan Firoz Shah, who was famous for building works of public utility, got a dam built and a causeway to join the tomb and fort, thus adding greatly to the attraction of both.

In its heyday, it must have indeed been a very pleasing sight and reminiscent of a paradisiacal tomb as it had the fort on the east, mountains to the west and Adilabad Fort on the south, with water coming from the north and lapping at the foot of the fort and the tomb complex. Sir Syed says that the tomb looked like a *katora* (bowl) in the middle of the water.

The waves in the water, the cool breeze and the greenery on the mountains reminds one of Paradise. The water here was the surplus from the Hauz e Shamsi in Mehrauli. As was the case of most monuments till early twentieth century, this too was occupied by villagers who had caused great damage to the monuments. However, it has since been repaired. Extensive repairs are being undertaken in the tomb complex and it is still very well preserved.

Mohammadabad/Adilabad/Imarat Hazar Sutun

Ab woh ghar ik veerana tha; bas veerana zinda tha
Sab aanken dam tod chuki thee'n aur main tanha zinda tha
Now this house was desolate; the desolation was alive
All inmates have long passed away; only I am alive

Juan Eliya

Mohammadabad/ Adilabad/ Imarat Hazar Sutoon

A thriving capital fort, whose lofty walls bear mute testimony to days gone by, is now a desolate place where few go. Sentries must have once protected the inmates but today most fear to enter for fear of being robbed or assaulted by miscreants in the lonely ruins.

Forming a triangle with the Tughlaqabad Fort and tomb is the fortress of Adilabad. Today it is known by the name of Adilabad but for many centuries it was called Mohammadabad. Sir Syed writes that Mohammad Tughlaq Shah killed so many thousands of innocents that the title Adil (just) slowly disappeared from his name and he was called Sultan Khooni. No one called him Adil and thus the name Adilabad fell in disuse.

This fort used to be connected to Tughlaqabad by a causeway but that is no longer extant. The portion where the lake must have been is a dusty bowl used as a playground by kids of neighbouring areas.

It is built in the same style as Tughlaqabad with huge blocks of stones, though not as grandiose. The entrance gate to the fort, however, is breathtaking.

The Palace of a Thousand Pillars, which was mentioned by Timur in his memoirs, was apparently inside this fort. It was called Imarat e Hazar Sutun and should not be confused with Qasr e Hazar Sutun built by Sultan Alauddin Khilji.

Sir Syed writes that the remains of this fort are on a small hill. It seems as if this building was made only as a leisure palace because to the south of Tughlaqabad is plain land where there used to be perpetual water. He built this palace just next to the source of this water body and a bridge to this palace from the city of Tughlaqabad; to the west of this palace, he made the tomb of Tughlaq Shah, building a causeway between these two as well. Further to the north of the fort walls he made the Imarat e Hazar Sutun with sandstone columns. This fort is now in ruins and there are no remnants of the columns or fort.

When I saw this palace I thought it was made as *baradaris* are built today. There is no doubt that this building was two-storeyed. In fact, it could even have been three-storeyed.[14]

Some people had confused this as the wooden canopy under which Sultan Ghiyasuddin Tughlaq died but that is wrong as that was built in Afghanpur by Sultan Muhammad bin Tughlaq as a prince and this was built after he ascended the throne.

The most graphic descriptions of Sultan Muhammad bin Tughlaq and his reign have come from Ibn Battuta, who since he received rewards and punishments in equal measure, had been very critical of the Sultan.

There are circular rooms that look like pits or dungeons in the fort which could have been used for punishment of whoever the Sultan considered guilty. I looked into one from the top and was suitably chastened and frightened at the thought of being locked away in this windowless room.

To the south was another fort known by various names such as Qila Shahenshahi, Dhobi ka Qila, Dahina Qila. It was a miniature version of Tughlaqabad Fort.

Surajkund/Lake of the Sun

Om bhūr bhuvaḥ svaḥ
tát savitúr váreṇ(i)yaṃ
bhárgo devásya dhīmahi
dhíyo yó naḥ prachodayat
We meditate on that most excellent radiance
of god Savitar (the divine stimulator/ vivifier),
who will/ shall inspire our prayers.[15]

According to Sir Syed, the fifth son of Anekpal, namely Suraj Pal, constructed this reservoir in 686 AD. However, General Cunningham places it in 1061 AD. This tank is still grand and a popular art and crafts fair is held every year near it, known as Surajkund Mela.

When it was built, this area must have been in complete wilderness and not so close to Lal Kot, the royal residence. It showcases the wealth, imagination and determination of the rulers of the past eras. Raja Suraj Pal was a sun worshipper and this lake was his dedication to the Sun God and a place of worship.

Suraj Kund

It is built in the backdrop of the Aravalli hills and is constructed in such a way as to form a semi-circular shaped embankment. It has been designed in the shape of a rising sun with an eastward arc. In the evening setting sun, this place has an epic look.

The first sight of this kund is breathtaking and reminds one of an Olympic sized amphitheater. Circular steps lead down to the bottom that is now dry. It used to spread over six acres of land when it was built and nestled in the hill between two districts called Lakkadpur and Baharpur. It was fed by water from nearby hills. Sultan Firoz Shah Tughlaq, the conservator, had the reservoir restored and the steps and terraces rebuilt with stones. Sir Syed also mentions that there was an ancient temple near the lake that was accessed by climbing fifty steps. Today there are just some roofless low walls there built by solid blocks of stone. There is a small entrance with only wilderness behind it; the temple has long since disappeared.

Sir Syed also mentions that a *garhi* (cave like structure) was built close to the ancient site of the Sun temple.

I had gone with Syed Mohammad Qasim, who is my fellow explorer in Delhi, and we decided to locate that. After many enquiries we were told that there was a Devi (goddess) temple nearby called Satkunda. After traversing dirt tracks we reached the temple, which is guarded by two stone lions. The temple was closed but we could walk around the complex. Just near the temple there were steps leading down to a tunnel. They were very dirty and not being sure of the safety of this tunnel, we desisted from going inside. Perhaps this was the *garhi*.

We came upon an ancient well, also called kund. Some local children had come to drink water from it and pray for success in their exams. On asking the few priests, we were told that a path led from here to the Surajkund Lake. We set off through the overgrowth, thorns and dirt. In a clearing in the jungle, some villagers were preparing a wrestling pit and a water tank.

It seemed as if we had stepped back in time and spent a pleasant fifteen minutes enjoying the scenery, the wilderness and the peaceful surroundings.

It was almost impossible to envisage that just a kilometre away in the Surajkund crafts fair there was a sea of humanity, bargaining for dress materials, wooden furniture, craftwork, paintings, enjoying cuisines from different Indian states and roaming around looking at wares from several participating states and countries.

When we entered the mela grounds there was a surreal feeling of continuity. Sir Syed has mentioned that in the month of Bhadon Sudhi Chatt, there is a big *nahaan* (ritual bathing) and a small fair is held.

While time moves on and things change, thankfully some things remain the same.

Kalka Devi Temple

Viran.cya[i-A]adi-Devaas-Trayas-Te Gunns-Triin
Sama-[A]araadhya Kaaliim Pradhaanaa Babhuubuh |
Anaadim Suraadim Makhaadim Bhavaadim
Svaruupam Tvadiiyam Na Vindanti Devaah
The trinity of Gods Brahma etc., (beginning with Brahma or right from Brahma) having worshiped your three Gunas became the Gods to whom Kali is Supreme. The Gods do not get your Natural Form (स्वरुपम॒) of beginning-less, prime among divinities, source of sacrifice, and cause of the universe (existence).[16]

As per Hindu mythology, millions of years ago, there were two demons named Simba and Nasba who gave a lot of trouble to the gods. Lord Brahma, to whom the gods complained, recommended that they pray to Goddess Parvati. When they did the *yagya,* a goddess, Kaushiki Devi, was born from the mouth of Goddess Parvati. Kaushiki Devi killed the leader of the demons Raktbhanch, but from the drops of his blood, which fell on earth, thousands of demons were born.

Then Goddess Kali was born from the eyebrows of Kaushiki Devi. Kali, 'whose lower lip rested on the hills below and the upper lip touched the sky above', drank the blood of the demons before it could fall on the ground as Kaushiki Devi slaughtered them. Thus Kaushiki Devi was victorious over the demons. In the end of *dwapar yug*, which was 4953 years ago, Kali Devi took up residence on this hill.

The temple we see today was built in 1764. Originally a vaulted *baradari* was built with the deity (which is an unfinished stone slab) enshrined in a marble enclosure. On her left side is an inscription with her name and date.

Sri Durga singh par sawar – 1821 Fasli
Sri Durga is mounted on a lion – 1821 Fasli

Kalka Devi Temple

The priests of the temple wanted a pinnacle made over the temple and, as they could not find anyone ready to undertake this task, they decided to let the Goddess give the orders herself. They made small chits with names of all the rich Hindus of the city and put it in front of the Goddess. The chosen one was Mirza Raja Kedarnath, who was the *peshkar* in administration during Emperor Akbar Shah's reign.

Accordingly in 1816 AD, Raja Kedarnath got the beautiful shikhara built over the vaulted structure with a 36-arched circumbulatory verandah around it. As soon as Raja Kedarnath's men completed the temple, people started building dharamshalas around it to accommodate devotees who came to the temples during the half-yearly fairs held here on *ashthami*, eighth of the month of Chait and Ashochki (Ashvim). These dharamshalas are still around with inscriptions on their facade giving nineteenth-century dates of construction and names of benefactors. Built in the late Mughal style, some of them are very attractive.

I spoke to one of the ladies who runs a stall selling offerings for the Devi. She has been living there for the past twenty-two years and has seen prolific construction activity in the area.

In front of the door of this temple are two red sandstone lions and a *trishul* (trident). As per Hindu faith, the lions pull the goddess's chariot and that's why they are stationed at the doorway.

The priest of the temple does pooja twice a day – in the morning and evening – and at 11 a.m. he offers *bhog* (offerings of food). The stone deity is covered by heavily decorated red cloth and there's a small, well-decorated bed kept inside the goddess's enclosure where she is said to rest at night. A ghee lamp is kept lit throughout the day on the enclosure. It is considered inauspicious if the lamp were to die out. When the prayers of the devotees and pilgrims are answered, they offer *chatr* (small canopies) and shamiana (cover) to the diety.

Dargah Hazrat Mahmud Bahar

> *O slave, if He should show His love to you,*
> *Love which His deeds perpetually renew,*
> *You will be nothing, you will disappear –*
> *Leave all to Him who acts, and have no fear*
>
> *Fariduddin Attar*[17]

Hazrat Syed Mahmud Bahar was a great scholar and saint and was a descendant of Hazrat Syed Nasiruddin Sonepati. He died in 1376 AD. Though his name is commonly spelt as Bahar, he was called *bahr*, meaning 'ocean', because he was a great scholar – an ocean of knowledge.

He is famous as the saint who revived a man from the dead: the story goes that there was an old widow whose beloved son had gone on a journey. She was his devoted disciple. One day the saint had a divine revelation that her son had died and only a pile of bones remained. The saint prayed to Allah and his prayer was accepted. The dead boy was revived and was united with his mother.

He was given the titles of Muhiyyul Izaam and Raja Haad Goad, along with another Badshah Ustakhwaanha (Emperor of Bones). His devotees had made a mud wall around the mazar. But today the saint's shrine has been remade in marble and tiles and is a very peaceful place. I spent some time in meditation there and felt a sense of peace.

The adjoining mosque is a famous and old one which has been renovated. Hazrat Nizamuddin Auliya would come to offer his Friday prayers in this mosque. There is a story told by Hazrat Nasiruddin Mahmud Chiragh e Dilli that Hazrat Nizamuddin Auliya used to walk regularly from Ghiyaspur to Kilokri. Once during summer when the hot winds were blowing, he passed by the Dargah of Malik Yaar Parra'n and felt dizzy due to the hot sun. As he was fasting that day, he had to stop at one of the shops near it where he wished for some conveyance so that he would not miss his Friday prayers.

The next day one of the disciples of Hazrat Nuruddin Malik Yaar Parra'n saw his Master in a dream. As per the sign from his master, he took a mare to Hazrat Nizamuddin Auliya as a gift but the saint, as was his habit, refused. He came again the next day and said that his Sheikh (Hazrat Nuruddin Malik Yaar Parra'n) had asked him to give it to the saint. The saint smiled and said that though the man's Sheikh had ordered him to gift the mare, his own Sheikh (Baba Farid) had not asked him to accept it. The third day the man returned with the mare, as his Sheikh had revealed to him that Hazrat Nizamuddin Auliya would accept it on the third day as his Sheikh had given him a nod to accept. Hazrat Nizamuddin Auliya accepted the mare and from that day onwards there was no shortage of horses in his *khanqah*.

Only the domed gateway in its compound survives in its original shape. It is in the Kilokri village.

Sarai Kale Khan

Humne bataao kis tapte suraj ki hoop se maani haar
Humne kis deewar e chaman ke saaye mein aaraam kiya!
Which scorching sun do you think defeated me?
Which soothing walls do you think protected me!

Sahba Akhtar

Sarai Kale Khan is today a busy bus depot and I doubt many know of its antecedents.

Emperor Sher Shah Suri built a chain of *sarais*, or inns, on Grand Trunk Road at intervals of two miles. These *sarais* were maintained at public expense and gave succour to all travellers. It was also an important point of communication as horse posts for quick change of horses for messengers were maintained here. This was possibly one of them. Though no traces remain today, it was built of rubble masonry and consisted of arched cells enclosed by an outer wall which were crowned by battlements. It is said that the name was given after a famous Sufi saint who is buried at the same location as the Delhi Airport. However, though the website Aulia e Hind mentions that a saint is buried in the premises of the airport, it doesn't state his name.

An article in the the *Deccan Herald* quotes the caretaker Bhagat ji, 'This mazar is a tribute to Bare Baba (Baba Kale Khan) and Chhote Baba (Baba Roshan Khan). Flights come and go but our saints are the ones keeping all the operations safe.'[18]

I haven't been able to make the connection as both this *sarai* and the airport are far apart but perhaps a devotee did the naming.

Panj Burja, Zamarudpur

Baad e fana fuzool hai naam-o-nishaan ki fikr
Jab hum nahin rahe, to rahega mazaar kya?

Why worry about your name and legacy after death
When I no longer be, how can my tomb remain?

Chakbast

During the reign of Sikandar Lodi, the Sultan of Delhi (1489–1517), a Jagir was given to an Afghan noble named Zamarud Khan in Kanchan Sarai and that area henceforth became known as Zamarudpur. His family was buried in the tombs there. There is a mention of the five tombs of Zamarudpur in recent years because of their state of deterioration and encroachment. There are some old reports that these tombs are to get a facelift due to the agencies of Indian National Trust for Art and Cultural Heritage (INTACH).

Having read these reports I decided to visit the area myself, not realizing the shock I was going to get!

Tomb 1: An Encroached Monument

An Encroached Monument

Maulvi Zafar Hasan had described the five tombs of Zamarudpur and said they were not in a very good state. I wonder what he would say about their condition today. As soon as we entered the village, I saw the first tomb boxed in by adjacent buildings but still standing tall. When I took out my mobile to click photographs, a local came out and told me I could not click pictures. He was extremely agitated and rude. Nevertheless, I stood my ground and managed to get a few shots though they weren't very good.

I don't know if these tombs are notified as there were no ASI boards anywhere to be seen. The entire area is also a Lal Dora, an unorganized settlement, and is exempt from building by-laws, construction norms and regulations, as specified under the Delhi Municipal Act.

Only the facade of the tomb was visible as it had been encroached on all sides. We could not see inside as the houses on either sides had taken over the entrances. They obviously don't encourage visitors.

Tomb 2: Monument of Desolation

A friendly lady in the park in front of the first tomb told us that there were two *gumbads* further down the road so we went into the lanes and peeped into what seemed like a blind alley, when I saw an old wall.

I was ill-prepared for the sight of a tomb filled with garbage and partially built upon. The lotus *kalasa* on the half dome peeping out was a favourite dumping ground for the high-rise tenement next to it. The tomb itself was closed on all sides and we climbed up the stairs of the tenement to get a better look. On the staircase I found a pillar peeping out. Maulvi Zafar Hasan says that it is a 16 square feet domed structure containing twelve dressed stone pillars. It was being used for residential purposes even back then and its pillars had been filled with earth.

Tomb 3: Monument being used as a cattle shed

We went further down into the narrow passages of the buildings that housed one-room apartments with a common toilet. One had another passage leading from it and I saw some old stones from afar when I entered. I ventured in to suddenly find myself in front of a huge dark cavern containing a white cow and yellow tarpaulin strung on four poles. A little girl passing by said it was indeed a *gumbad* and that a handicapped man lived in it with his cow. The old man in question came along and, seeing us taking photographs, kindly turned on the light from a precariously hanging switch. This was the largest of the five tombs and had been neatly divided into corners. The old man lived in one corner with his cow and a battered tin box holding his meager possessions. It was so crowded and dirty that we could not go in. Maulvi Zafar Hasan described it as a tomb measuring 27 feet 5 inches

A monument being used as cattle shed

square, constructed of dressed stone and surmounted by a rubble plastered dome. On the north, south and east are recessed arches enclosing three arched openings, which give access to the interior, while the west has three mihrab recesses. A doorway in the south mihrab gives entry to a winding staircase leading to the roof. The dome is octagonal with a red sandstone finial. Inside there are three graves. It was being used as a residence back then with the pillars filled up with earth.

It was too full of garbage and dirt for us to explore the interiors so we accessed it from another side and discovered another row of single rooms on four levels with common bathrooms at the end of the passages. Here we met a scrap seller living there on rent. This side was heaped with scraps and a broken doll on the top seemed very symbolic.

Tomb 4: Monument of Neglect

Monument of neglect

Three tombs had been found in heartbreaking condition and we were now more or less prepared for the worst. We started peeping into a few lanes in the general area we had been told to look in. From one narrow lane we glimpsed what seemed an old stone pillar. The lane suddenly opened onto a square with a *baradari* on a high plinth with the look of a busy dhobi ghat. Once again we climbed on to the top of the six-storey tenement one-room apartments, a common toilet on each landing and a tap attached to a small wall for washing and cleaning.

The top showed an elegant lotus finial with wild growth all over it. From the top floors we could see some of the surviving medallions that had Allah written on them in Arabic.

Maulvi Zafar Hasan described it as measuring 22 feet 5 square inches, standing on a plinth of 7 feet in height. It consists of a domed pavilion with twelve pillars in dressed stone. Traces of blue tile decoration are found on the battlements that crown the roof and on the octagonal roof of the dome. The dome is ornamented on the inside with incised plaster and intersecting bands of red colour.

We were trying to find a way to enter the pavilion and saw a kid climbing a staircase adjoining it on the opposite side. So we set off there and climbed in. Remnants of the incised plaster and calligraphy with the *kalima* written on it were visible and the floor had all kinds of garbage strewn over it; it was being used as a garbage dump-cum-store-cum-laundry room.

Tomb 5: Buried amidst buildings

I don't think anyone else in recent times had found all five tombs but we were determined to do so. Once again we went back to the shopkeeper and found an old gentleman who said there was one behind the row of buildings in front, so we set off to that alley. There was a passage running behind the buildings; we entered it but came back out on to the road without finding any

Buried amidst buildings

trace of a tomb in there. An old lady was passing by and we asked her about the *gumbad*. She said that it had been enclosed from all sides by buildings but we could find a part of it peeping out in a narrow lane in front of us. It was a tiny passage next to a fancy house and in complete darkness. It didn't seem old from afar but as we came close we could make out an old column support on the side. There was no way we could go any closer to it as it was surrounded by garbage and unused stuff.

Stepping out, we asked a shopkeeper if we could go up to get a bird's eye view from one of the buildings there. When he assured us it was not a problem, we climbed up the six floors. This one was in a slightly better condition with students staying in it. We reached the *barsaati* of the building and peeped over the edge of the inner wall. As if in a deep well, we saw a dome peeping out with tall bricked walls on its four sides. I realized why no one had found it till now and along came the sad realization that soon it may not be there to find.

Maulvi Zafar Hasan described it as a domed structure, hexagonal in plan with a diameter of 16 feet and containing six dressed stone pillars. In the centre of the dome is a grave of rubble and plaster. Today there are no traces of any pillars or grave. The level of the ground has come up to the dome.

Basti Khan ki Baoli

Magar jab shukr e ne'mat mein jabin jhukti hai bande ke
Woh sachi bandagi hai ik sharifana ita'at hai
When a man prostrates in grateful thanksgiving
That is true devotion; true piety

Josh Malihabadi

Tomb of Basti Khan

Khwaja Sara Basti Khan was an important noble in the reign of Sultan Sikandar Lodi. Though today it's in a limited area but he had enclosed an extensive piece of land near Hazrat Nizamuddin *basti* and built a mosque, *baoli* and tomb in it with an impressive gateway as entrance. The tomb was built in 1488 AD. The *baoli* dried up centuries ago but the gateway, tomb and mosque survive despite many additions.

The gateway is a white building with a lofty dome and soothing to the eyes. It is built of stone and mortar, measures 35 square feet and stands on a plinth. It was locked so we could not see inside but we were told it was a store room now. There is a madrasa and mosque attached to the gateway that covers up most of the area of the complex. It was neatly lined with wooden benches for holding books and bookcases – the Quran and other books were kept in it.

Since it was a winter afternoon when we visited, prayers were being held in the warm winter sun on a cemented courtyard. At the side of the courtyard is a small tank for ablutions, which could possibly be built on the remains of the *baoli*. The original mosque is inside a covered portion and is a simple three-bay mosque, neatly kept and with painted decoration on the ceiling and mihrab. The facade has been enclosed with a small door leading inside and has changed considerably from the time it was built. It is a peaceful place where Syed Mohammad Qasim and I said our afternoon prayers in quiet solitude and thankfulness.

A double staircase in the courtyard leads to a pretty, white-coloured gateway through which one enters the upper portion. The tomb itself stands on a raised terrace and contains five arched cells in each of its four sides. The dome is white while the rest of it is painted a bright red. It measures 21 square feet and its height is 60 feet.

The four corners were marked by red *chhatris* of which only one remains. Internally, the dome was lined with red sandstone and ornamented with alternate circular bands of white and black marble. Not much of the marble remains.

When we visited it, we found the tomb full of wooden planks and leftovers from construction activities. There were no signs of the grave, which is supposed to have been in the middle. Today it serves as the Jama Masjid of Defence Colony and is well maintained with a busy madrasa.

III

Mubarakpur Kotla

Tomb of Sultan Mubarak Shah

Tomb of Sultan Mubarak Shah

Aap sochaa hii kiye, us se miluu'n yaa na milu'n
Maut mushtaaq ko mittii mein mila bhi aayi
You kept contemplating to meet or not to meet
Death was eager, annihilated the ardent in the ground

Fani Badayuni

Sultan Mubarak Shah ruled from 1421–1433 AD. On 31 October 1432 AD, he laid the foundation of a city on the banks of the River Yamuna and the name given to that 'ill-omened'[19] city was Mubarakabad. He devoted much time and care to the direction of this building.[20]

He was assassinated in 1433 AD and buried in the village of Mubarakpur. Today one sees only a beleaguered tomb, imprisoned inside iron railings and surrounded by buildings on all sides. However, once upon a time this was an open space with a compound wall and entrance gate.

It is an octagonal tomb built of local quartzite stone and is a very attractive monument of the same style as Isa Khan's tomb. There is a twenty-four-column gallery around the tomb, covered in soot and dirt, and the lotus floor at the entrance, which is so similar to the one on Sultan Muhammad Shah Sayyid's tomb in Lodi Gardens, is a wilted one. One can only guess the colours that must have adorned it once upon a time.

I noted down some lines from a description of the tomb written by Carr Stephen in 1876, just so we could heed it as a warning of our mortality no matter how many permanent structures we seek to build.

> This is built in the midst of a large yard, surrounded by a stone battlemented wall. The gates leading into this court have the side posts and lintels of grey stone and are oblong in shape except at the top, where the side posts project in the usual fashion. The actual doorway is a narrow line of plain blue encaustic tiles, and below are two full-blown lotus flowers in white marble. A short approach from this gate leads to the tomb itself, a massive octagonal building, constructed of the grey stone of the country. It stands on a plinth approached by an ascent of two steps with a sloping way of stone in between. The tomb is surrounded by a covered colonnade with 24 pillars, standing at the edge of the plinth. These pillars are of a highly peculiar form, being oblong, and so cut as to present the appearance of two oblong shaped pillars joined by a narrow belt, at each corner of the octagon, the outer pillar is strengthened by a buttress of solid stone, which greatly contributes to the general appearance of strength and solidity which characterize the building.
>
> The dome springs from a low cylinder ornamented with colour and with sixteen finials. The dome itself is crowned with an open octagonal lantern of red-stone, around the dome are eight octagonal cupolas resting on low pillars. There is only one door to the tomb, that to the south. In the space between the lintel of the doorway and the apex of the arch, in which it is set, is a fanlight of latticework in stone. The other six apertures except the west one answer to this south doorway, except that the doorway in their case is filled up with stone lattice work, divided by two horizontal bars of solid stone. The west side is filled up with a handsomely carved qiblagaah, also in stone.[21]

However, the buildings all around it have blocked any light into the tomb and the *qiblagaah* remains dark. We tried to see it using light from our flash cameras but it's grimy like the rest of the tomb.

All I could make out was that there are five tombs, which too had not been left in a respectful state as I could make out a mound of used disposable paper plates and cups, which were probably remnants of someone's picnic. The grave under the dome is of a man, with graves of two women on the right and a row of graves of children – two boys and two girls – near the doorway.

The way to identify male and female graves is that male graves have a raised design called *qalam* and female graves have a flat slate type design called *takhti*.

This tomb was used as a residential area pre-1924 and smoke spoiled the marble cenotaphs.

I talked to one of the boys who lives nearby who said that they got the tomb opened by ASI after they wrote to the former Lt Governor of Delhi Jagmohan Malhotra as they wanted to look after it and pray to the man buried there, who is considered the patron 'Dada Pir' or saint of the area. Like his father before him, he looks after the cleanliness and maintenance of the tomb. They belong to the clan of Bainsla Jat, who own most of the houses in the area. When I pointed out that it wasn't very clean, he said they sweep it on Thursdays when their womenfolk come to offer sweets and flowers on the graves and light incense sticks.

Whatever may be the reason, I quite understood why making permanent grave structures is forbidden in Islam.

Mubarakpur Kotla Masjid

Paani paani shahr-panaah
Masjid mandir sab paani
In ruins lies the city of refuge
Desolated stand the houses of worship

Khalid Karrar

Mubarakpur Kotla Masjid

This mosque is at a short distance from the tomb of Sultan Mubarak Shah. Its access has been encroached upon and one can reach it only through the tenements that have sprung up all over. It is difficult for someone who has not been there earlier to reach it.

We had to jump into it over a pile of garbage. Local kids were playing cricket in its courtyard. The mosque is in a terrible state and was occupied by a dog and her litter who didn't allow us to enter.

The mosque has a five-arched structure and is three-domed with a double bay. It is made of local quartzite. The spandrels are ornamented with circular discs containing the *kalima* incised in plaster in Tughra calligraphy. They are still there, staring defiantly through the ruins.

I climbed up the steep and dilapidated steps to check out the domes. There's a central one, which can be seen from below, and two smaller ones.

It was already encroached in 1919 when Basheeruddin Ahmad wrote his book and he said that Manikchand Baqqal, who has his house nearby, considers it his own property and has shut off all other entrances except the one which goes through his own foyer.

Moth ki Masjid

Moth ki Masjid (Courtesy: ASI archives)

Ghar se masjid hai bahut duur chalo yu'n kar lein
Kisi rote huye bachhe ko hansaya jaaye
The mosque lies far away from the home
Why not bring a smile on a crying child's face

Nida Fazli

This mosque is inside a village of the same name and one can make out its beauty and grandeur from the remnants. It has a magnificent gate with marble bands of calligraphy however; like the rest of the structure, it is not anywhere near its original glory.

There is a famous legend written in *Khulasat-ut-Tawarikh* that one day Sultan Sikandar Shah found a grain of *moth* (pulse) in the Jami Masjid. He picked it up and handed it over to his wise and sagacious minister, Miyan Bhoiya, who paid obeisance and took it. The minister thought that since the grain had the honour of being touched by the Sultan, he should ensure that it received everlasting fame. He accordingly sowed it in an orchard attached to his house and the plant that grew yielded 200 grains. He kept repeating this process till he had a full harvest in a few years and built this mosque from the proceeds of selling that harvest. Later, he informed the Sultan about his labours and invited him to recite his prayers in the mosque, which was hereafter called Moth ki Masjid.

Sir Syed writes that there is an inscription on the red stone inside the well. Its letters have crumbled but it seems clear from the remaining ones that this mosque was built during the reign of Sultan Sikandar Bahlol in approximately 1488 AD. Today that well is sealed so one can't see what's inside it.

It is built in the Lodi-era style of architecture of a five-arched facade with the central one being larger than the rest. The central doorway is set in a lofty recessed arch. The pilasters of these arches are ornamented with small recessed arches. There are eight such arches in total, one above the other, and five on the side arches.

The building is disfigured in places from inside and one can only imagine its lost grandeur. It comprises of a single bay with mihrab niches in front of the arches on the western wall.

It has three domes of stone and mortar in the regular Lodi style. There were coloured plastered medallions used for decoration but as the villagers of Mubarakpur used it for residential purposes, the soot from their cooking fires has ruined them. In fact, Carr Stephen described the condition in 1876 when it was occupied and said that the villagers had built mud partitions inside the mosque to divide it into small rooms.

Chote Khan ka Gumbad

Teen Burj:
Bade Khan ka Gumbad, Chote Khan ka Gumbad, Bhure Khan ka Gumbad

Kyun hamein maut ke paighaam diye jaate hain
Ye saza kam hai ke jiye jaate hain
Why keep on reminding me of death?
Isn't it enough of a punishment that I live!

Shamim Jaipuri

These three tombs stand inside a park in the residential area of South Extension I, very close to Mubarakpur Kotla. Bade Khan and Chote Khan are next to each other. These are not the names of the persons buried here and seem to be the result of someone's imagination based on size of the tombs. They belong to the Lodi era and there is extensive calligraphy done on all three. The Chote Khan ka Gumbad has exquisite incised calligraphy on its doorways as well as in the arches inside. Yet, there is no clue about the identity of the person buried here. There are two possibilities: either that there was no headstone with the name or that it was stolen. The tomb of Bhure Khan has been cut off from the other two because the land in between is under the control of a private company. Since there is a litigation underway, the tomb of Bhure Khan has been cordoned off by barbed wire.

All three tombs are square buildings with single domes springing out of narrow cylinders. Low ornamented parapets protect the roofs. As the name suggests, Bade Khan ka Gumbad is considerably larger in size and has five graves inside whereas Chote Khan ka Gumbad has only one.

According to Sir Syed, these seem to be in the Lodi style of architecture, so were probably built around 1494 AD during Sultan Sikandar Lodi's reign. The narrow cylindered neck of the domes is very typically Lodi. They were probably important nobles of the Lodi era to build such magnificent tombs. Today it is a popular place for rest and recreation. When I visited the tombs, the local village ladies were sunning themselves. One of them told me she'd been visiting the premises for the past forty years to sun herself in winters.

Kale Khan ka Gumbad

Waada kar ke aur bhi aafat mein daala aap ne
Zindagi mushkil thi, ab marna bhi mushkil ho gaya
Your promise has added to my woes
Life was as it is difficult, now I can't even die!

Jaleel Manikpuri

Its name has come from its appearance, since before restoration it had become black. It has four main doorways and two smaller ones on each side of the bigger one. The dome measures 22.5 feet from inside and 42 feet from outside, suggesting a double dome structure.

Kale Khan ka Gumbad

There are two graves inside it. The western mihrab has Quranic ayat inscribed on it. All the arches have spandrels with the *kalima* in Tughra style of calligraphy. It is on a plinth of 2 feet 3 inches. The central grave is unusually high. It's in a well maintained garden, providing a nice meeting and resting place for youngsters and people living nearby.

Darya Khan's Tomb

Shaame'n kisi ko maangti hain aaj bhi Firaq
Go zindagi mein yu'n mujhe koi kami nahin
The evenings yearn for someone, Firaq
Though life seems to go on

Firaq Gorakhpuri

This is also in South Extension I and at walking distance from Teen-Burj. It's in a picturesque garden and is always full of youngsters and people who enjoy greenery.

When the Lodi chiefs built their tombs, I am sure they would never have thought that one day they would provide succour to families living in concrete jungles!

The grave is on a 90 square feet platform that is 8 feet high and accessed by twelve steps. The grave itself is on another circular platform in the centre and is flanked by four *baradaris* (pavilions).

Only one pavilion is in a somewhat acceptable condition. The rest are in various stages of deterioration with damaged domes. Each dome is inscribed with Quranic ayat on the inside.

Darya Khan's Tomb

Gumti of Sheikh Ali

Gumti of Sheikh Ali

Aish se kyun khush huye, kyun gham se ghabaraya kiye
Zindagi kya jaańe kya thi aur kya samajha kiye
Why let luxury lull you or sorrow worry you
Who knows what life is and we think it to be

Moin Ahsan Jazbi

This is an octagonal pavilion with eight arches of red sandstone. There used to be three graves inside it, which have been removed though at what point one doesn't know. It is set inside an enclosed garden and is a haven on hot summer days; however, entry is restricted here as it is the RWA office of Defence Colony. It is 18 square feet with 9 feet × 5.5 inch arches. I know it's not haunted or we would have heard of it. Maybe Sheikh Ali likes the company.

Monuments Inside the Jawaharlal Nehru Stadium

Hai meri zillat hi kuchh meri sharaafat ki daleel
Jis ki ghaflat ko malak rote hain wo ghaafil hu'n main
My insult is a testimony to my goodness
I am that negligient one, for whose carelessness, angels weep

Allama Iqbal

This stadium was built by the Government of India to host the 9th Asian Games in 1982. It is a multipurpose sports arena, hosting football and other sporting events as well as large-scale entertainment events. The stadium is also home to three monuments.

Phuta Gumbad

It is a bit odd to find a Lodi-era tomb nested into an ultra modern structure but the Phuta Gumbad is exactly that. At some point before a makeover, its dome must have broken down to give it this name.

The structure is built on a raised platform. It is of a square plan with arched entrances on three sides and a closed wall (a mihrab recess) on the fourth (west) side. The dome springs from an eight-sided drum. The interiors of the tomb are decorated with arched niches and squinches. Externally, the features to be noted are the *kanguras* on the drum wall, the lotus crest on the dome and the high plinth.

Phuta Gumbad

Sixteen-sided Tomb

Though it's the Phuta Gumbad which is more famous, to me it was the flat sixteen-sided tomb near Gate no. 1 that I found very interesting and attractive.

A Lodi-era monument, it stands on a platform. Each of the sixteen sides has a deeply recessed arch. There is an entrance on the south but with bats flying around, it was impossible to enter.

Sixteen-sided Tomb

A short flight of stairs leads to the top, which has some more unknown graves. All these monuments were repaired during the Commonwealth Games in 2010.

Unknown Tomb

An unknown tomb stands in front of Gate no. 14. It's in a bad state and quite unattractive. The only interesting feature is its dome in the shape of an octagonal *chhatri* (umbrella).

IV
Jahanpanah

Khirki Masjid (Courtesy: ASI archives)

Wiraana e Dehli mein jo gaya, ek fakhta mujhse yu'n boli
Paigham tujhe ek deti hu'n, sun ai ghaafil ku ku meri

Yeh wiraane jo dekhte ho maamoor thay abaadi se kabhi
Yahan shahr bhi thay, baghaat bhi thay, basti thi kinaare ju meri

Go charkh falak ki gardish se ruposh na huyi mehfil apni
Hai aaj ke din tak mutajassas yeh chashm nazaara ju meri

Shaaho'n ke muqaabil ko dekho, ibrat ke manaazir ko dekho
Eent eent mein qasr e Jamshedi hai, dekhti aankh har su meri

Thaa shor jahan takbeero'n ka, hungame thay jarraro'n ke
Ab aalam hu hai, chaar taraf baaqi hai faqat ku ku meri

Nit rang naya hai duniya ka maayoos na ho ai bekhabro'n
Kahti hai yeh ku ku meri, kahti hai yeh ku ku meri

I visited the wilderness of Delhi and there a dove spoke to me
I give you a message, O Negligent One! listen to me!

This wilderness, O traveller, was once a populated, flourishing city
There were gardens and towns beside the river, can you hear me?

The cycle of destiny changed everything, and all my joy was gone
My sight yearns for that sight until now, woe is me!

Look at the city that was acquainted with the kings once, and now a sign of destruction
Palaces of ancient Iranian kings in every broken brick of this city, are seen by me

Here once was the sound of Allah ho Akbar, and slogans raised by soldiers
Today, it's just silence or my voice. Heed you me

Do not despair, O people! For this is how the colours of the world change with time.
That's what says this dove, can you hear me?[22]

Jahanpanah was built by Sultan Muhammad bin Tughlaq (1325–51 AD) between 1326–27 AD in the empty area near Mehrauli, Siri and Tughlaqabad. His intention was to enclose the area from Qutub Delhi to Siri within its walls, giving it the name Jahanpanah or 'refuge of the world'. It was abandoned when Sultan Muhammad bin Tughlaq ordered the shifting of the capital, along with its inhabitants, to Daulatabad.

Walls of Jahanpanah

The walls of Jahanpanah were constructed in around 1328 AD by Sultan Muhammad bin Tughlaq. There were six gates in the western wall and seven in the eastern: but the name of one only survives, the Maidan Gate on the west, near an old *idgah*. Emperor Sher Shah removed the walls of this city to build his city, Shergarh.

Khirki Masjid

Wo masjid ghar na ban jaaye kisi ka
Namaaze'n band hain khaali padi hai
Alas! That mosque may become someone's residence
No longer are prayers held there, what echoes there is silence

Sardar Asif

I have had many discussions with heritage enthusiasts on the name of this mosque as I disbelieved that such an impressive mosque could be named after its rather ordinary windows. On reading *Asar-us-Sanadid* by Sir Syed, my belief was found to be true.

He writes:

Near the famous Satpula dam, there used to be a village in ancient times, which was called Khirki. On this location Khan e Jahan Firoz

Shahi built a mosque at the same time as the dam was being built. This mosque has become famous by the name of the village, Khirki.

As in the case of a famous cantonment in Pune of the same name, the word Khirki meant that the area so named was a window into another region. It also meant that, just as in Shahjahanabad, it also contained a postern gate. As the village lay just within the southeastern wall of Jahanpanah, both possibilities could be correct.

Built in 1387 AD, it is a double-storeyed, square mosque measuring 288 feet. There is an underground storey, or *taikhana*, which is 11 feet in height but is now closed to the public. This *taikhana* had over 100 vaulted cells. The upper storey is 22 feet in height and is strengthened on all four sides by 45 feet high sloping, domed towers. The gateway is flanked by two massive monolithic columns and is very impressive. The interior isn't open like other mosques of the period and has covered arcades that open out into four open courts. There are twenty-five equal squares divided into nine compartments with low vaulted roofs. In every square there are symmetrically arranged columns grouped together. These support the flat roof, which has groups of nine domes rising from it. There are nine groups of nine small domes, one group in the middle, one at each corner and one in the centre of each side, making it a total of 81 domes. Counting the one over each of the three entrance-gateways and the fourth over the prayer-niche to the west, the total number of domes is 85. Though quite a few are damaged now it's still an impressive sight when one climbs upstairs. The four domes on the northeast side were destroyed in the nineteenth century because of a fire ignited in the heap of grass kept there. Till the 1920s, the villagers used this mosque for residential purposes.

There are heavy, not particularly attractive sandstone grills near the windows in the outer walls. There are a total of 180 columns.

Hindu architecture is represented by heavy door lintels and the dripstones around the courts supported by lintels on brackets, also shown in the photograph. Altogether this mosque is well worthy of an inspection.[23]

It's a pity that such a magnificent mosque lies in obscurity near Select Citywalk Mall. As its entrance is blocked by the houses that have sprung up all around it, not many know of its existence.

Satpula

Satpula

Qisse se tere, meri kahani se zyada
Paani mein hai kya aur bhi paani se zyada
More than your tale, more than my yarn
What lies in these waters, watching the waters turn

Abrar Ahmed

This is a dam made by Sultan Muhammad bin Tughlaq in 1326 AD to regulate the force of a stream which ran through the city Jahanpanah. It was built in the eastern wall of that city and is one of the few monuments which testify to that ill-fated genius's vision rather than his more infamous caprices, as it was meant to promote agriculture. The city was reeling under severe economic crunch due to natural and manmade calamities and this was one way to bring in more area under cultivation thus alleviating famine-like conditions.

The dam consists of seven stone and masonry arches about 38 feet high, which gave it the name Satpula. As it fell into disuse and a madrasa came up in the rooms inside the doorways in later years, it was also referred to as a madrasa. The dam itself is 177 feet long and has two towers of 39 feet width, flanking it on each side. The towers must have been defensive bastions and are shaped like *darwazas* with a small octagonal room in each corner of the tower where the madrasa flourished. There are arched openings with steps leading to the top of the dam.

There are many legends attached to the waters of this dam, the chief being that Hazrat Roshan Chiragh e Dilli had once come here and, as the time for *asr* (afternoon prayers) was ending and he couldn't find water to do ablutions, he dug up the ground with his bare hands and water started spouting. He did his *wuzu* (ritual ablution for prayers) and blessed it, saying that whoever had a bath in this water would be miraculously cured of all disease.

According to Sir Syed this is a tale woven by the *khadims* of Hazrat Roshan Chiragh e Dilli to earn money by cheating ordinary people who come here.

Sir Syed believes that the *khadims* call this a miracle and have made small holes in front of these arches to sell the water to people, even though the water from these holes isn't pure for *wuzu* as per shariah. He adds that no reference to this incident has been found in any book and even if it is true, it is not a miracle.

In the nineteenth century, according to Sir Syed, Muslims made this hole a pilgrimage spot and bathed the sick in its waters since they considered it as sacred as Ganga Jal (water of the Holy Ganges). Today, locals are unaware of any stories or legends related to this dam. It is on Press Enclave Road and close to Saket.

Tomb of Hazrat Yusuf Qattal

Tomb of Hazrat Yusuf Qattal

Khada hu'n zer e falak gumbad e sada mein Munir
Ke jaise haath uthaa ho koii duaa ke liye
I am standing under the sky in the dome of sound, Munir
Like a supplicant beseeching God with raised hands

Munir Niyazi

This dargah is by far the prettiest I have seen. It's like a vermillion mark of spirituality on the surrounding area. Though very small, it is exquisite and very well preserved.

The grave inside is painted green; this adds to its aura of spirituality but the fresh white and green on the mihrab wall is very jarring. I wish its caretakers had left it in its original condition.

Hazrat Sheikh Alauddin, the grandson of Baba Farid Ganj e Shakkar, built this tomb for Hazrat Yusuf Qattal during the reign of Sultan Sikandar Lodi in 1497 AD.

Hazrat Yusuf Qattal was a disciple of Qazi Jalaluddin Lahori. He came to Delhi from Lahore and was an important personage in the Lodi court. According to Maulvi Zafar Hasan, he performed 'religious devotion' at Satpula. It is possible he may have played an active role in the madrasa there. As was the custom, it may have been built in his lifetime as his dwelling place and later he was buried there.

It has a small dome, measuring 18 feet 2 square inches, supported by twelve pillars which are filled in between by exquisite pierced stone screens with geometric designs while the pavilion and lattice screens are of red sandstone with a lime mortar dome. The dripstones are carved to represent tiles, encaustic tiling was used to decorate the cornice round the dome, and one can catch glimpses of blue. A small white-painted mosque stands closeby. It is in a shabby condition. There are ruins of a building at the entrance, which may have been a *khanqah* or madrasa. It must have been very elegant and attractive when it was built and may be the inspiration for the tomb of Imam Zamin near the Alai Gate under the Qutub Minar. Both are very similar.

The locals have traditionally been very devoted to this dargah and even today they offer flowers, incense and *halwa* on Thursdays. They refer to him as Pir Baba. A group of boys were playing cricket there and one of them spoke to me. Anoop said he had grown up here and that his parents were also among Pir Baba's devotees. On Holi they come and offer colours here. This dargah is near Khirki village.

Dargah Hazrat Roshan Chiragh e Dilli

Dargah Hazrat Roshan Chiragh e Dilli

Hungama garm hasti na-paayedar ka
Chashmak hai barq ki, ke tabassum sharar ka
The tumult of the ardous, undurable life
Is it a wink of the lightening or a smile of a spark?

Sheikh Ibrahim Zauq

Sheikh Nasiruddin Mahmud was the last great Chisti saint of Delhi and the Khalifa or successor of Hazrat Nizamuddin Auliya.

There are three legends connected to his being given the name Chiragh e Delhi or the Illumined lamp of Delhi.

Sir Syed wrote that when Hazrat Makhdoom Jehanian Jehan Gasht was performing umrah in Mecca, he was by asked Hazrat Abdullah Yafai, who was the saint in Delhi these days. Makhdoom Sahab replied that the in these days the lamp of Delhi is illuminated by Hazrat Nasiruddin Mahmud.

The other legends are that one-day many mendicants were sitting with the Mahboob e Ilahi Hazrat Nizamuddin Auliya. Hazrat Nasiruddin also came there. His teacher asked him to sit down but he said, 'My back would turn towards them,' upon which the Mahboob e Ilahi replied, 'A lamp has no back.'

The one that is the most popular relates to the time when Sultan Ghiyasuddin Tughlaq Shah was building the city of Tughlaqabad. The Sultan, angry that the workers were working at nights on the *baoli* of Hazrat Nizamuddin Auliya's dargah, stopped the supply of oil to it.

When Hazrat Nizamuddin Auliya came to know of it, he asked his disciple Hazrat Nasiruddin Mahmud to put water in the lamps and burn them. The order was obeyed. From the day, Nasiruddin came to be known as Roshan Chiragh e Dilli.

However, in light of Prof. Mohammad Habib's assertion mentioned above that the contemporary historians don't refer to any dispute between these two eminent personages, it is possible that neither of the two stories given above may be true and the last a later-day fabrication.

Hazrat Nasiruddin Mahmud Roshan Chiragh e Dilli was stabbed to death by a fanatical Jalandari fakir who had come to him to beg for alms on Friday, 18th Ramzan in 1356 AD. He was eighty-two years old.

Sultan Firoz Shah revered the saint in whom he reposed great faith and served him sincerely. He had a dome added to the chamber in which the saint lived and it in this room where Hazrat Roshan Chiragh e Dilli was buried, alongwith his most revered possessions: his cloak, staff, cup and prayer rug, which had been given to him by his Pir-o-Murshid, Hazrat Nizamuddin Auliya.

Hazrat Roshan Chiragh e Dilli did not approve of *sema mehfils*, though he never specifically banned them, and that it why, unlike in other *Chisti* dargahs, one does not find qawwalis being sung here.

He was also a poet who wrote exclusively in praise of Allah. The dargah stands inside an irregular oblong enclosure. While Emperor Muhammad Shah built most of the enclosure in 1729 AD, the domed gateway was built twelve years after the death of the saint. The gateway is built of stone masonry with an arched door. The room inside the gateway is 31 square feet and has masonry *chabutras* on either side of it.

The shrine itself is a single room, supported by twelve pillars surmounted by a masonry dome with a gilt pinnacle. The dome is plastered and rises from an octagonal drum.

Several additions have been made in the shrine complex from time to time. At present there are several structures in the complex like the assembly hall (Majlis-Khana) or the assembly hall (Mahfil-Khana), apart from many graves and tombs of eminent personalities inside the enclosure. There are also several mosques in the dargah enclosure. King Farrukhsiyar built one among them in the early eighteenth century to pay homage to the great saint. A new mosque has been rebuilt recently at this location.

To the east of the shrine of Hazrat Roshan Chiragh e Dilli is the tomb of Khwaja Tahir in a latticed enclosure. It has a marble headstone. There are two *gumbads* from the Lodi era but the identity of the people buried there is unknown. His *urs* is held on seventeenth Ramzan. There is a wooden takht measuring 7 feet x 4 feet and 3 feet high made from a single piece of wood. It's elaborately carved. Dakhni Beg sent it and it has a verse carved on it.

Takht chobi niyaz Dakhni Beg, ba Janab Nasiruddin Mahmud
Quddisa sirru hul azeez 1143 AH
(Dakhini Beg has presented this wooden throne in the service of his holiness Nasiruddin Mahmud, May Allah illuminate your grave)

According to legend Hazrat Khwaja Banda Nawaz Gesu Daraz, who was the disciple of Hazrat Roshan Chiragh sent this piece of wood. It is possible that he may have used the name Dakhni Beg as he had gone to the south and established his *khanqah* there.

Emperor Muhammad Shah had got an enclosing wall built around the area at an expense of 3.75 lakh rupees. One can see the Doorways to it at the entry points but otherwise it is no longer there.

There is an ancient khirni tree in the courtyard of the dargah in front of the domed gateway, which is a very pleasing sight. According to legend it dates back to the days of the saint himself.

The area is known after the famous saint. Dargah of Chiragh e Dilli is located in the Chirag Delhi Village and can be reached by either taking the Lal Bahadur Shastri Marg through the Chiragh main road or the Outer Ring Road through the Soami Nagar South Colony.

Tomb of Sultan Bahlol Lodi

Jism yu'n rooh se laga kahne
Tan se jab hoke beqarar chali
Chod kar saath ek umr ka aaj
Haif ai jaan e gham gusaar chali
The body lamented to the soul
In a state of restlessness do I leave you
We lived together for an age
Alas! No longer can you comfort me

Unknown

When Sultan Bahlol Lodi died in Mauza Badhaoli near Saket in 1488 AD, he was buried near the dargah of Hazrat Roshan Chiragh e Dilli. His son Sultan Sikandar Lodi built this tomb. This tomb adjoins the western wall of Dargah of Hazrat Roshan Chiragh e Dilli. It was earlier set in the salubrious environs of an orchard, known as Jodh Bagh, but today it has been encroached from all

Tomb of Sultan Bahlol Lodi

sides and is barely managing to survive. It is possible that it was a summerhouse of the king during his lifetime. Around the mausoleum is now an extensive cemetery. It is a 44 square feet chamber with three arched openings each on three sides and surmounted by five domes, the central one being larger than the others. The western wall has two openings and the third arch is the qibla mihrab, which is closed and decorated from inside.

The arches are decorated with Quranic inscriptions and medallions in their spandrels. There were stone eaves on top of the arches out of which only parts have survived. The grave is attractively decorated. Emperor Babur writes in his memoirs that he visited the garden where tombs of Sultan Sikandar Lodi and Sultan Bahlol Lodi were situated, though it is hard to believe that Sultan Bahlol Lodi ever had a garden to himself for his eternal rest. Sultan Sikandar Lodi has been luckier as he has an entire garden named after his dynasty!

Dargah of Hazrat Sheikh Salahuddin Dervish

Duniya hum ne sara e fani dekhi
Har cheez yahan ki aani jaani dekhi
I saw this world as a temporary abode
Everything here was in a transit mode

Unknown

Sheikh Salahuddin was the khalifa of Suhrawardi saint Sheikh Sadruddin, who was the son and successor of Sheikh Bahauddin Zakariya of Multan.

Sheikh Salahuddin Dervish came to Delhi during the reign of Sultan Muhammad bin Tughlaq and faced state persecution as he opposed the Sultan's scheme of shifting the capital. He died in 1339 and was buried near the Khirki village. He was a contemporary of Hazrat Nasiruddin Mahmud Roshan Chiragh e Dilli.

Dargah of Hazrat Sheikh Salahuddin Dervish

The dargah has close similarities to the Tughlaq style and was built during the reign of Sultan Firoz Shah in 1353 AD. There are two graves inside it, both of which don't have headstones so they can't be identified. There used to be marble screens between the pillars supporting the dome, very similar to that of Hazrat Yusuf Qattal's dargah, but now there are no traces of that. The eaves surrounding it have, however, mostly survived.

A new mosque has been built on the site of the medieval one and the whole complex is inside a boundary wall. Since the trustees of the mosque do not encourage visits to the dargah, though it is clean and neat, it has no signs of any offerings or the smell of incense or candles.

There used to be a jungle on this spot, known as Jungle of Sheikh Sallah; however, only a small patch of green remains and most of the trees have been replaced by a concrete jungle.

This dargah is in the Green Zone of Savitri Nagar. The area around it must have been considered sacred, as can be seen from the remnants of graves in the trees and bushes. Car mechanics and labourers now occupy it. Two broken down *gumbads* within the mosque complex have had their centotaphs removed and are used as store rooms and dump yards.

Dargah of Hazrat Sheikh Alauddin Nurtaj

You are my protection O Lord, my salvation:
grant to Farid the blessing of Your adoration.

Baba Farid[24]

The dargah of Sheikh Alauddin (died 1541–42 AD), grandson of the famous Sufi saint Baba Farid Ganj e Shakkar, is in Sheikh Sarai. His father was Sheikh Nuruddin Ajodhani and he was a disciple of Qazi Jalaluddin of Lahore. He is famous as Alauddin Ajodhani.

Dargah of Hazrat Sheikh Alauddin Nurtaj

There used to be an enclosed compound with his dargah in the middle. The *gumbad* is lofty and attractive. It is a 28 square feet building with its entrance on the east. There are three rows of two plastered graves inside. Twelve lattice screens are built in the walls. The grave with the railing is of the saint. The other five graves are of his relatives.

Bismillah ar Rahman ar Rahim and the *kalima* (Islamic creed) are inscribed on the doorway. Bands of intricate written inscriptions run on the ceiling of the dome, which are ayat ul kursi in the first and the last three ayat of Surah Hashr in the second. The ninety-nine names of Allah and titles of the Prophet are inscribed in the third band. There are decorations on either side of the lattice screens too.

They are other small pavilions with domes that rest on twelve pillars. The pillars have some magnificent red sandstone latticework screens between them. However, there are some individual features. The tomb of Sheikh Alauddin is somewhat more ornate than that of Hazrat Yusuf Qattal. It has coloured and chiseled plaster symbols on the arches and parapets. Bands of intricate written inscriptions run on the ceiling of the dome. The tomb of

Hazrat Yusuf Qattal is comparatively smaller but enchanting nonetheless and its dome is encircled by encaustic tiles.

This dargah is in the alleys of Sheikh Sarai and has been sadly encroached upon. The people living around it do not like outsiders and it is therefore difficult to visit it. This is one monument I couldn't visit personally and my description is from the books I've consulted and a description by Syed Mohammad Qasim who visited it to take photographs.

Dargah of Sheikh Kabiruddin Auliya

Selflessness is the sign of the selfless;
Bow down at the door of the selfless.
The selfless are of the highest authority,
The kings of the time and the wearers of the crest and crown

Rupa Bhawani[25]

Dargah of Sheikh Kabiruddin Auliya

Sheikh Kabiruddin Auliya was the son of Hazrat Yusuf Qattal and a disciple of Hazrat Roshan Chiragh e Dilli. His dargah is quite close to his father's dargah in Sheikh Sarai.[26]

It was famous as Lal Gumbad as it is made of red sandstone. Its marble decoration on the gateways and sloping walls resembles the tomb of Sultan Ghiyasuddin Tughlaq Shah.

There is a famous legend attached to this dargah. It is reported that some thieves came to steal the golden finial. As there was no staircase, they fixed iron stirrups on the western wall to scale the top. However, they could not succeed in their nefarious mission as they fell down from the top and were blinded. Two of the stirrup rings still remain, giving the monument another name: Rakabwali Gumbad. It is believed that if one looks carefully, we can still see their bloodstains near the rings. I didn't find any though.

The compound is quite big with three wall mosques, another small gumbad – it was locked but houses an unknown tomb and innumerous graves scattered all over. It seemed like a very popular spot. Women from nearby houses were soaking in the winter sun and children were playing football and cricket.

The entrance to the tomb has a wooden door in a dilapidated condition. The guard didn't have the keys but from the lattice screens, we could see rows of graves inside.

Some distance from the Lal Gumbad is a very small pavilion standing on an octagonal platform supported on four pillars. It has a fluted dome made from a single stone.

Below it used to be a tiny cell, only three feet wide, and almost filled up with soil. This is believed to be the abode of Kabiruddin Aulia, who spent his day under the *chhatri* and night in the cave. Near it was a well, which had the date of 1410 AD.

It used to be famous as the Banjara ka Gumbad as people thought some *banjara* or gypsy had got it built. Today it is known as Kharbooze ka Gumbad

Kharbooze ka Gumbad

because of its shape. It is now inside the Rainbow Montessori School and seems completely disconnected with the Lal Gumbad. I saw it from outside as the school gates were locked and we couldn't go inside.

This gumbad is in Panchsheel Park South.

Bijay Mandal

Ye aur baat ki Akhtar haveliya'n na rahi'n
Khandar mein kam to nahin apni aabru roshan
It's a different matter that mansions remain no more
Still our reputation shines through the ruins

Sultan Akhtar

Jahanpanah, the fourth medieval city of Delhi, was built in 1326–27 AD by Sultan Muhammad bin Tughlaq (1321–51 AD) to address the constant threat of the Mongols. It was a fortified city (meaning in Persian: 'Refuge of the World') but today all we have are descriptions by the Moroccon traveller, Ibn Battuta, who lived in Delhi during Sultan Muhammad bin Tughlaq's reign. Sultan Muhammad's palace had three gates; each furnished with a flurry of officials presided over by marshals in caps of gold plumed with peacock feathers. The first gate was also home to the executioners. The second led into a large *mashwar*, or audience chamber. 'The third door,' wrote Ibn Battuta, 'opens into the immense and vast hall called *Hazar Sutun*,' which means [in Persian] 'a thousand pillars.' 'The pillars are of painted wood and support a wooden roof, carved most exquisitely ... It is in this hall that the sultan sits for public audience.'[27] The famed treasure house in this palace, which housed the riches captured by the Sultan from his conquests as well as taxes from citizens, is now a pile of dirt. Locals say they used to discover gold coins till recently.

Bijai Mandal

Once upon a time there used to wells filled with treasures in this area. Today one can find dirt and broken beer bottles lying around.

Sir Syed calls this the Badih Manzil. Note: Badih Manzil here means extraordinary or unique, not big. It is written as बड़ी. It is an octagonal building with a diameter of 38 feet 3 inches and is 20 feet high, built of rubble with steeply sloping sides, the corners being strengthened by dressed stones. At each of its four cardinal points is a doorway. The roof is reached by some stinky and dirty stairs. At the south-west corner are three circular holes of diameter 1 feet 5 inches, which look as if a cover was fitted in them. They are filled with dirt today.

According to Sir Syed, it supported a structure, probably a *baradari* crowning the *mandal*. It is possible from the holes present that there was a canopy supported by wooden or stone pillars on top of this structure.

The purpose of the *mandal* is unclear and, according to Akhbarul Akhyar, it was a *burj* (bastion) of the fort of Jahanpanah and it was from this strange architectural wonder that the Sultan inspected his troops.

The entire structure is built on a raised platform, surmounted by another higher platform. Some of the rooms are inaccessible to the public and could possibly have been the living quarters of the Sultan.

Bijay Mandal is an important piece of history lying in utter neglect, state of disrepair and isolation. When we went there, it was a public holiday and there were groups of boys chilling all around. They said that here they got the privacy to eat and drink as they pleased.

Legend has it that Sultan Firoz Shah built a tunnel that went from this spot all the way to Hauz Khas. The guards on duty have often pointed to an area opposite the unknown tomb/gateway as being the location of that tunnel.

There is an unknown tomb to the west of Bijay Mandal, just next to it, which is probably from the Lodi-era. This is the first thing that greets you as you enter the fabled city. It measures 31.5 square feet. It was probably a tomb

Qasr e Hazar Sutoon

but there is no grave inside it. It has two doorways on each side but the ones on the east have been plastered and closed.

During the reign of Sultan Sikandar Lodi, a saint by the name of Sheikh Hussain Tahir came to Delhi and was accommodated in this Bijay Mandal on royal orders. He passed away in 1503 AD and was buried here. His dargah is a small open shrine with graves of his relatives around it. There seem to be remains of a madrasa opposite his shrine. It is in the Kalu Sarai Village.

Qasr i Hazar Sutun

Jisko dekho wahi zanjeer-ba-paa lagta hai
Shahr ka shahr huwa daakhil e zindaan Jaana'n
Wherever the eye goes one sees shackled people
It seems the entire city has been sent into a prison, Beloved.

Ahmed Faraz

After Sultan Alauddin Khilji had completed building the city of Siri in 1303, he built a palace, which he named *Hazar Sutun* (thousand columns). As per legend, the heads of thousands of slain Mongols were buried in the foundation of this palace too.

General Cunningham placed this palace in the western portion of Siri, Qasba Shahpur, towards the west.[28] J.D. Beglar, however, found some ruins of this palace outside the southern walls of the city of Siri.[29] But as per the commonly held belief, the Qasr i Hazar Sutun was in the premises of Bijay Mandal as many stone slabs have been found here with holes in them for holding wooden poles or columns.

This palace witnessed many events such as the murder of Malik Kafur, Sultan Alauddin Khilji's counselor. Khusro Khan murdered Sultan Qutbuddin Mubarak Shah (Sultan Alauddin Khilji's son and successor) here. Khusro Khan then sat on the throne and was executed on the very spot where he had murdered his predecessor, on the orders of Sultan Ghiyasuddin Tughlaq.

Tariq e Firoz Shahi says that in the same year Tughlaq Shah 'seated himself in the Hazar Sutun and, in the presence of assembled nobles, wept over the unhappy fate which had befallen Qutbuddin and other sons of Alauddin his patron.'[30]

Some confusion arose from the fact that Timur confused this palace with the Imarat e Hazar Sutun that was built by Sultan Muhammad bin Tughlaq inside Adilabad.

Begumpur Masjid

Har shakhs yahan gumbad e be dar ki tarah hai
Awaaz pe awaaz do sunta nahin koi
Every one here seems like a dome without doors
You call and call again, but no one hears

Mohsin Zaidi

Begumpur Masjid

Begumpur was the name of a medieval village which contained many monuments from that era. However, very few remain today and the most prominent of them is the mosque close to Bijay Mandal.

From childhood I have been hearing a phrase:

Khandhar bata rahe hain ke imarat shaandar thi
The ruins testify to the monument's magnificence

I was almost in tears when I saw the ruins of a once magnificent place of worship and piece of architecture.

Begumpur is the Jami Masjid of Jahanpanah, the fourth city of Delhi built by Muhammad bin Tughlaq. Jahanpanah was built to fight the Mongol menace. Except for some ruins not much of the city survives today.

Today it lies in the heart of Delhi, near Malviya Nagar, in a state of neglect and disrepair.

Though many historians and websites say that these mosques (or some of them) were built by Khan-i-Jahan Maqbul Tilangani (Malik Maqbul), the ASI Publication *Delhi and Its Neighbourhood* says '[...the Begumpuri-Masjid, [is]... reputed to have been built by Khan e Jahan Juna Shah...' Even Sir Syed in his seminal work *Asar-us-Sanadid* attributes the Begumpur Masjid to Khan e Jahan Firozshahi (Junior).

The famous mosques made by the Khan e Jahan father-and-son duo are:

- Khirki Masjid
- Begumpur Masjid
- Masjid Kalu Sarai
- Kalan Masjid (Hazrat Nizamuddin basti)
- Masjid Firoz Shah Kotla
- Kalan Masjid (Turkman Gate)
- And as per Hearn, the Chauburji Masjid on the ridge

There is a dispute whether Tilangani was indeed the builder of these mosques, but I am going with the public view.

There is a lofty and impressive gateway on the east with fifteen steps on each of the three sides to take you inside. This beautiful facade is, however, spoilt as I have often found the locals playing cards on or around them. There were two other gateways on the north and south but they are no longer in use and the steps leading up to them have been destroyed. The eastern and southern gateways are set in the wall of the mosque and protrude about ten feet out of it.

Once inside, the visitor is greeted by the sight of a huge courtyard with prayer corridors on three sides. This mosque was earlier paved with red sandstone.

Andhero'n mein khandar sota pada hai
Abaabiilo'n ke lashkar jaagte hain
The stones lie desolate in the darkness
While flocks of swallows stay alert

Unknown[31]

The mosque measures 307 feet × 295 feet and included within its walls is a madrasa and a treasury, with the courtyard measuring 247 feet × 223 feet.

The central *pishtaq* is supported by pylons on both sides and houses the central mihrab. In Islamic architecture, a *pishtaq* is a rectangular frame around an arched opening and is usually the formal gateway to the *iwan* or square hall.

There were villagers living inside along with their cattle till 1921, when the ASI evacuated them. However, they continued to use it as a dumping ground and a common toilet. The present-day state of disrepair bears testimony to it.

It was built in the austere style of rubble masonry. Sir Syed describes it as strong and ugly. No doubt it is sans any embellishments we are used to seeing in medieval buildings, but to me there is grandeur in its starkness.

One feature of the mosques from the period of Sultan Firoz Shah is the presence of multiple domes. Though many here are broken, one can still see a row of domes on the roof. They provide convenient seats for locals and tourists today.

The mosque contains sixty-four domes, the central one being a height of 9 feet. The Begumpur Masjid is known as the first Indian example of the 'Brhatmukhi' mosque type; at the centre of the 24 arches on its main facade, an extremely large arch stands out, flanked by massive tapering pylon-minarets.

There is another smaller structure with mosque-like mihrabs attached to the main one. It is said that it was a ladies' mosque but its name, Mallu Khana, and the fact that it has no separate entrance makes me think it could have been a madrasa. The locals today use it as a toilet. I had to cover my nose to overcome the stench there and, having failed to see clearly in the dark, stepped on filth and dirtied my shoes. I cannot describe my feelings at seeing such deep disdain for our architectural heritage and places of worship.

Sarai Shahji and Maqbara Sheikh Farid Bukhari

Hazar shukr ki hum ne zabaan se kuchh na kaha
Yeh aur baat hai ke poocha na ahl e duniya ne
A thousand thanks that I didn't utter any complaint
It's another matter that the world never bothered to ask!

Nasir Kazmi

This tomb is in Sheikh Sarai and, though it is in a very bad state and the gate is kept locked, I am mentioning it because of the role played by Sheikh Farid Bukhari. One has to walk a bit towards the east, inside the mohalla near Begumpuri Masjid, to access it.

Sheikh Fariduddin Ibne Syed Ahmed Bukhari was given title of Murtaza Khan during the reign of Emperor Jahangir. He was a prolific builder and built a *sarai* and jailhouse. He was the Mir Bakshi in Emperor Jahangir's rule and was devoted to him. He played an important role in the suppression of Prince Khusrau's revolt after Emperor Akbar's death and defeated the young prince on the banks of Beas. The title of Murtaza Khan was given to him in light of this victory.

He was also the Governor of Gujarat and later Punjab. He died in Pak Pattan in 1615 AD; his body was brought and buried in Begumpur.

His grave is made of marble with a beautiful headstone. There are ruins of an old monument near his grave, which has some more graves and galleries. Despite being in ruins, it is quite an impressive double-storeyed building. Locals use it as a residence. Just near it is an old *sarai* known as Sarai Shahji.

Tomb Stone Sheikh Fareed Bukhari

Kalu Sarai Masjid

Kal ki baat aur hai main ab saa rahu'n na rahu'n
Jitna jee chaahe tera aaj sata le mujhko
Tomorrow is another day, I may not remain this way
Torment me as much as you want to today

Qateel Shifai

Kalu Sarai Masjid

This mosque was also built by Khan e Jahan Firoz Shahi. It is quite close to Begumpur Masjid and, since mosques should be a certain distance apart, the proximity of the two denotes that Kalu Sarai may have been an important habitation once upon a time and thus deserved its own mosque.

It is built of rubble with plaster on top. It had seven arched openings in the facade of its prayer hall, most of which have now collapsed, and is surmounted by a series of low domes in the Firoz Shahi style. It measured 73 feet in length.

V
Firozabad

Jami Masjid, Firoz Shah Kotla

Dil o Dilli dono'n agar hai kharaab
P'a kuch lutf us ujde ghar mein bhi hain
Both heart and Delhi may have been damaged,
But some small pleasures still remain in these ruins

Mir Taqi Mir

Sultan Firoz Shah Tughlaq is known as India's first conservationist and builder. He not only built many hospitals, *sarais*, mosques and palaces but also repaired older structures such as Qutub Minar, Hauz Khas and the tombs of Sultan Iltutmish and Sultan Alauddin Khilji. He had added sandalwood *chaparkhats* (canopies) to the tombs.

According to Basheeruddin Ahmad, he is said to have built 40 mosques, 30 madrasas, 20 *khanqahs*, 200 *ribaat* or *sarais*, 30 cities, 100 reservoirs, 40 dams, 100 palaces, 150 bridges and countless gardens in his reign of thirty-eight years and a few months.

The Sultan, having selected a site on the banks of the Yamuna at the village of Gawin, founded the city of Firozabad (1354 AD) before he went to Lakhnauti a second time. Here he commenced a palace and due to the nobles of his court having also obtained houses there, a new town sprang up five *kos* away from Delhi'.[32] The city was a half-hexagon in plan with its base facing the Yamuna River, going upto the ridge in the north and Hauz Khas in the south.

As was the custom in those days, Sultan Firoz Shah Tughlaq reused the stones and materials from the older cities.

Siri, Jahanpanah and Qila Rai Pithra were stripped and left desolate to build and populate a new city. Traders' animals were sent to the old cities to bring a load of stones to Firozabad. The city would have extended within a radius of approximately two kilometres. The limits of the city of Firozabad are difficult to trace because the city of Shahjahanabad was next to it, with a part of the older city included within. The stones from Firozabad were used for building Shahjahanabad, leaving most of it in ruins.

It seems probable that Firozabad was probably a collection of suburbs, with no city wall. This is verified by the fact that when Timur invaded, the old cities of Siri and Jahanpanah, which were held against him, were walled cities.

The areas included in Firozabad were:

1. Indrapat
2. Sarai Sheikh Malik Yaar Paraa'n
3. Sarai Sheikh Abu Bakr Toosi
4. Village of Gawin
5. The land of Khetwara
6. The land of Lakhrawat
7. Andhawali
8. Sarai of Malika
9. Bulbuli Khana, which houses the tomb of Sultan Raziya
10. The land of Bhari
11. The land of Mahrola
12. The land of Sultanpur

This document also provides important authentication that Sultan Raziya's tomb is indeed in Bulbuli Khana and not in Tonk or Kaithal as many entries in public domain claim.

The first building to be built was the Sultan's palace or Kotla. Other nobles built their mansions around it.

Firozabad was filled up with houses and mansions from Indrapat (Purana Qila) to Kushk e Shikar on the ridge. It had a population of about 1.5 lakh.

There were eight public mosques and one private mosque. The public mosques could hold congregations of 10,000 people each. The city included three palaces, hunting lodges and various other monuments.

Tughlaq's chief architect was Malik Ghazi Shahna and his deputy was Abdul Haq. There were superintendents for the artisans. Very few traces of the city remain today, which as per Shams Siraj Afif's description, would have been double the size of Shahjahanabad. The city of Firozabad was a very popular resort and people from the older cities of Delhi would come here for pleasure. We can recreate the city in our mind by imagining Shahjahanabad.

Kabuli Darwaza/Lal Darwaza/Khooni Darwaza

Zauf mein taanaa e aghayaar kaa shikva kya hai
Baat kuchh sar to nahin hai ke uTha bhi na saku'n
In weakness why should I complain of others taunts
After all they are mere words, not my head which I am unable to lift
Mirza Ghalib

This Darwaza has been given many names but the one in use nowadays is Khooni Darwaza.

I have driven past Khooni Darwaza many a time as it's very close to Firoz Shah Kotla, a favourite haunt of mine, but one day I finally decided to explore it. Not many know that this gate was built by Emperor Sher Shah Suri for his city Shergarh (Purana Qila area) and was named Kabuli Darwaza because, it according to Maulvi Zafar Hasan, caravans to Afghanistan passed through it to the northern gate of Emperor Sher Shah's city.

At least till 1919, when *Monuments of Delhi* was published, it was called Kabuli Darwaza or Lal Darwaza because of the red stone used.

Khooni Darwaza

The facade of the gate is imposing; it measures 53 feet 5 inches in width and has a height of 50 feet 9 inches from base to top of the parapet. It's built of Delhi quartzite. This gate is now fenced in with its own patch of wilderness and wild grass and few who pass by know of its gory past.

The reputation of this gate was already bloody to start with, since it is said that Emperor Jahangir had the two sons of Abdur Rahim Khan e Khana'n, a minister in his father Emperor Akbar's court, killed and hung on this gate. Khan e Khana'n had supported the claims of Emperor Jahangir's son, Khusrau, who was also Emperor Akbar's favourite against Emperor Jahangir, and he paid the price later. It is said that Emperor Aurangzeb also displayed Dara Shukoh's head here after he had him killed in the War of Succession.

The name Khooni Darwaza alludes to the cruel and unprovoked act of Major Hodson on 22 September 1857 when he was taking the sons of the Mughal Emperor, who had surrendered to him in Emperor Humayun's tomb, to Red Fort. These were Mirza Mughal, who had been the initial leader of the Mughal troops against the British, and Mirza Khizr Sultan and his grandson

Mirza Abu Bakr. As the procession went towards the fort, citizens of Delhi with joined them white cloth tied on their heads (*kafan baandh kar niklay hain*). Near Kabuli Darwaza, Hodson panicked, fearing an attack against himself and his hundred-odd men. He felt that the rescue of the princes may overturn the tide against the British, who had subdued the 'mutiny' after much bloodshed and effort, and shot the princes in cold blood.

Qila Mualla ki Jhalkiyan by Arsh Taimuri, a descendant of Bahadur Shah Zafar, gives a description by Mirza Qumqamuddin, who was present on the occasion.

He writes that when Major Hodson arrested Mirza Mughal, Mirza Khizr Sultan and Mirza Abu Bakr and put them in a bullock cart to be transported to the Qila, the cart driver ran away in fear, excusing himself on the pretext of wanting to relieve himself. The cart driver was replaced by Mirza Mughal's special attendant, Hussain Mirza.

According to Mirza Qumqamuddin, the writer of *Muzaffarnama*, when the cart was approaching the jailhouse, Major Hodson stopped it and asked, 'Who is the commander-in-chief?'

Mirza Mughal replied, 'I am.'

Hodson made him alight from the cart and shot him at point blank range. After that, he came back to the cart and asked, 'Who is the colonel?'

Mirza Khizr Sultan said, 'I am.'

Hodson made him get down and shot him in the same way.

The bodies of these two princes were writhing in the dust with fountains of blood spouting from the wounds. Mirza Abu Bakr, unable to see the state of his uncles, called out in anger and Major Hodson came to him, dragged him down and shot him too. The first bullet hit his arm and the next on his thigh; he fell down on the third.

When the corpses were cold, one of the riders with Hodson hacked off the heads and set off with them.

Tomb of Abdur Rahim Khan e Khana'n

Namaz in Jamaat Khana of Hazrat Nizamuddin Auliya Dargah

Bhuli Bhatiyari ka mahal

Emperor Humayun's tomb (shot at sunrise)

Inside a tomb in Zamarudpur

Minar e Zarrin at Firoz Shah Kotla

Wazirpur tombs

Lal Bangla in Delhi Golf Course

Dargah Hazrat Yusuf Qattal

Design in Masjid Qila e Kohna

Petitions to the jinns at Firoz Shah Kotla

Astana of Hazrat Nizamuddin Auliya Dargah

Tomb of Darya Khan

Jami Masjid at Firoz Shah Kotla

Tomb of Sultan Ghiyasuddin Tughlaq

Begumpur Masjid

Mirza Qumqamuddin wrote that he was sitting in the rath, shivering with fear and waiting for his turn, but Hodson ignored him and, leaving the rath behind, went off with his cavalrymen and the heads of the princes.

Hodson took their naked bodies to Chandni Chowk, where they were left to rot in the sun in front of the kotwali for days. He was later censured for this by the British authorities but by then the barbaric deed was already done.

Today, the gate is kept locked after a student of Maulana Azad Medical College was raped at the same location in 2002.

It is built on three levels with staircases leading to the top. The different floor levels of the gate are marked by windows framed in red sandstone, each furnished with a balcony carried on heavy quartzite corbels.

According to Maulvi Zafar Hasan, 'Heavy kangura battlements, rubble built and dressed with grey stone, crown the parapet of the gate and the string course immediately below them, being broken over the central arch by three damaghah intended for the vertical discharge of projectiles or boiling oil.'

It seems so innocuous and innocent from afar but even during the Hindu-Muslim riots of 1947, many refugees were killed while they were proceeding towards Purana Qila for shelter through this gate.

Kotla Firoz Shah

Na Sikandar hai na Dara hai na Qaiser hai na Jam
Be-mahal khaak mein hain qasr banana waale
Neither Alexander, nor Darius, nor Caesar or Jamshed remain
The builders of palaces under the open skies in dust are lain

Barq Mirza Raza

To any cricket fan, the name Firoz Shah Kotla is very familiar. Who can forget the thrill of watching Anil Kumble take ten wickets in a single innings in that stadium! So it did not come as a surprise to me that my driver drove me to the

stadium instead of the fort when I asked him to take me to Firoz Shah Kotla. He had no clue that there was an old fort after which the stadium was named and so had to ask around for directions.

Firoz Shah Kotla, the ruins of Delhi's fifth city, lies on Bahadur Shah Zafar Road. Sultan Firoz Shah Tughlaq built this city on the banks of Yamuna in the village of Gawin in 1354. It was originally called Kushk e Firozabad and later changed by the British to Firoz Shah Kotla, or Firoz Shah's citadel.

Though very few structures survive inside, it was used as a prototype for later Mughal fortresses as this is the first time the concept of a Diwan e Aam for the public and a Diwan e Khas for the nobles was introduced.

On his return to Lakhnauti and Jajnagar after a victorious campaign, he lamented the lack of a historian to record his triumphant return. Barani had died, so the Emperor took it upon himself to write about it. Shams Siraj Afif notes in his *Tarikh e Firoz Shahi*:

> Among his other qualities, he had a remarkable fondness for history. Just at this time Mauláná Zíáu-d dín Barní, the author of the *Tárikh-i Fíroz Sháhí* died, and the Sultán expressed to every learned man the great desire he felt for a historical record of the events of his own reign. When he despaired of getting such a work written, he caused the following lines, of his own composition (az zabán-i khwesh), to be inscribed in letters of gold on the walls (imárat) of the Kushk-i Shikár-rav, and on the domes of the Kushk-i nuzúl, and the walls (imárat) of the minarets of stone which are within the Kushk-i Shikár-rav at Fírozábád:—
>
> I made a great hunt of elephants, and I captured so many: I performed many glorious deeds; and all this I have done That in the world and among men; in the earth and among mankind, these verses may stand as a memorial to men of intelligence, and that the people of the world, and the wise men of the age, may follow the example.

However the quality of the verse may be, when the Sultan writes, the world reads! ASI published a memoir written by J.A. Page, the superintendent in 1937, which reconstructs the Kotla on the basis of its ruins. I describe it based on his account.

The main entrance is to the west and is surrounded by a series of low one-storeyed chambers, most of them in ruins with only the rear walls remaining. These served a dual purpose, with the chambers being used as a guard room and the roof serving as a terrace from which the loop holed upper walls of the Kotla could be manned.

These guard rooms also converted the polygonal outline of the exterior fortified walls into a simple quadrangle inside, with an entrance court accessible from the front gateway via an open passage.

Today, these chambers are guarded by the pigeons which enliven all old buildings in Delhi. There are bowls of water and feed for them.

In front of it was a colonnaded *dalan* where visitors would wait. Most of the place is in ruins and one has to use their imagination quite vigorously. On a Thursday, when the grateful come to fulfil their *mannat* and bring huge *deghs* of *zarda*, it is once again full of people waiting in line to take their share. That is described later in the chapter.

Just after the guard rooms and before the palaces is a small niche, blackened by the oil and soot from lamps lit by devotees of jinns and brightened by rose petals. This is the niche of Nanhe Miyan, one of the most important jinn saints of the Kotla. This corner is always full of petitions written by devotees. Many of them ask for his intercession in solving their problems, which can be as diverse as prayers for a relative who has been imprisoned, financial aid for marriages, quick resolutions for problems with in-laws, lovers asking for help to get married as well as blessings sought via wedding invitations.

From here one enters into a huge grassy square with sentry boxes on the sides. We come to know from Afif's *Tarikh e Firoz Shahi* that there were three palaces where the Sultan sat in the state. The first was known as *Mahal e Sehan e Gilin* (the Palace of the Clayey court). Another name for it was *Mahal e Angoor* or Palace of the Grapes. This was for the reception of high nobles, dignitaries, officials and distinguished literary men.

The second palace was *Mahal e Chajja e Chobin* (Palace of the Wooden Gallery) and was used for the reception of principal personal attendants.

The third was the *Mahal e Bari Amm* or Palace of the Public Court, also called *Sehan e Miyanagi* or Central Quadrangle. This is the last building in the sequence and some of it is still standing. It was used for general receptions by Sultan Firoz Shah but today it is believed to be the abode of jinns and there are mendicants sitting there dispensing *taveez*, charms and advice on Thursdays. This is called the 'Dher waale Baba ka mazar' as one regular visitor, Guddu, told me that there used to be mound of rubble which was the grave of a jinn-saint and has now been levelled by ASI. A white mark demarcates the area where flowers, incense and sweets are offered. There is a wall with threads with multiple messages and letters to jinns hanging on it. These contain entreaties for meditation and prayers. Candles and incense sticks are always burning at its base.

These palaces were whitewashed and decorated with paintings of sceneries and portraits forbidden by the Sultan as they were considered against the tenets of Islam. He also forbade the nobles from wearing silk and golden brocades as both are frowned upon in Islam. However, every Friday after public services, parties of musicians, athletes and storytellers from the four cities of Delhi would come to the palace. Though he was a very pious and devout Muslim, he had a weakness for wine, which he drank in complete privacy. Once, during a campaign in Bengal, he was discovered with his wine cups by his general, Tatar Khan, who came in unannounced. Thereafter he gave up drinking wine.

From Shams Siraj Afif we also come to know of a *Tas e Ghariyal* or plate bell which was invented by the Sultan and placed at the top of the *darbar* of the Kotla; this was a source of awe for people. He was greatly loved by his people and performed great acts of charity as well as built institutions for public welfare.

The Riverfront and Royal Palaces

Dil ki basti bhi shahr e Dilli hai
Jo bhi guzra ussi ne loota
My heart is like the city of Delhi
Whoever passed through, looted it

Khwaja Mir Dard

The ruins of the citadel indicate that the royal apartments and palaces were situated on the riverfront. This is the area on the right and centre of the Kotla, towards the river end (now a garden on a lower level).

This plan was later followed by the Mughals in Agra but Delhi was considered the most pleasant and desirable spot.

A detailed illustrated plan was drawn by J.A. Page. The *zenana* palace was located here. There is a beautiful circular *baoli* near the Masjid but it is now out of bounds for the public due to an unfortunate incident a few years ago. There are rooms on two tiers around the well, which has been enclosed in a steel grill. This became famous as the *pariyo'n ka kuan* (the well of fairies). Even today, many women come to light diyas, incense sticks and offer flowers and sweets to the fairies. Though Anand Vivek Taneja mentions in his book *Jinneology* that the jinn-saints are overshadowing the fairies increasingly.

It does not matter what time of the day you go there, you will see incense sticks, diyas and candles burning in various nooks and corners, even in the underground areas.

Baoli of Firoz Shah Kotla (Courtesy: ASI archives)

Jami Masjid, Firoz Shah Kotla

Jami Masjid, Firoz Shah Kotla

Dilli ke na thay kuche, auraaq e musawwar thay,
Jo shakl nazar aayi, tasveer nazar aayi.
The lanes of Delhi weren't streets but the work of an artist
Every face that I saw was a masterpiece

Mir Taqi Mir

The other notable building in the Kotla is the Jami Masjid, the congregational mosque. It was built by Sultan Firoz Shah's Prime Minister Khan e Jahan in 1354 AD and is one of the seven mosques he built.

It was so grand that Timur offered prayers and read a Khutba there, ordering a similar one to be made in Samarqand. It is said he even used the same artisans and labourers for this purpose.

Not much of it remains today except for the entrance, steps and some part of the walls. The masjid was to be repaired in 1847 when a committee was formed to make plans for the same. However, the war of independence in 1857 put its implementation on hold indefinitely.

The mosque has been designed in such a way that the enrance door faces the north and not east as was the norm in mosques. This is because the River Yamuna flows on the east side, very close to its eastern walls.

The square-domed *darwaza* which still survives is very grand and is a popular subject for photographers. It is built on a high plinth with steep steps leading up to it. One enters a huge courtyard surrounded by walls. The presence of recesses indicates that there must have been arches and windows along the entire length of the walls.

There were staircases in the north and south walls running from the underground madrasa cells to the top which also gave access to the mosque. There seem to be remains of a well for ablutions in the middle of the mosque. That well has now been closed. However, the 1847 committee raised doubts that it could have been a shaft sunk to support the foundation of the dome erected over it.

The dome of this mosque is described as having been octagonal with marble slabs on its eight sides, on which the *Futuhat e Firoz Shahi* was engraved, very fitting as it was opposite Ashoka's Pillar. Though no traces of the dome remain, the 1847 Committee of the Archaeological Survey of India found six of the eight capitals peculiar to pillars supporting domes lying around the mouth of the well/shaft.[33]

There is said to have been a bridge which connected it to the pyramidical structure with Ashoka's Pillar but no traces of it remain.

Once upon a time, the side small domes must have covered the aisles; today they are no longer extant. There are imams appointed by the Delhi Waqf Board to lead prayers here and they can usually be found in one of the niches in the wall. It is a functional mosque and prayers are offered here daily. I happened to be there on a Thursday afternoon and prayed with the congregation.

Ashoka ka Laat /Ashoka's Pillar

Ashoka ka Laat/Ashoka's Pillar

> *Dekhna hai to mujhe dekh main kaisa hu'n*
> *Mere ujde huye ghar baar ki jaanib mat dekh*
> *If you want to look, see how I am*
> *Don't glance at my ruined house*
>
> *Azhar Abbas*

The antiquarian that Firoz Shah Tughlaq was, he saw two Ashoka pillars during his travels and ordered them to be brought to Delhi. The one in the Kotla is from Tobra, near present-day Ambala.

An eyewitness account from *Sirat e Firozshahi* (from a text composed in 1370 AD) says:

> … in the village of Topra, by the banks of the Jatan, stood the stone pillar, the likes of which in height and circumference had not been seen by anyone… The sages and wise men of the time were simply astonished at the sight, and though they dived deep into the sea of thought they succeeded not in bringing out the pearl of the solution of these secrets – namely whence and

> how this heavy and lofty stone monolith was brought to this place and what were the exact engineering methods employed in its erection here. Verily such an achievement could hardly have been accomplished by human beings for the simple reason that it is beyond the power of Man.

According to Maulvi Zafar Hasan's *Monuments of Delhi*, a bed of 'senwal' silk cotton was made to cushion the pillar when it was uprooted from its old position, so that it had a soft, cushioned fall. The cotton was then removed carefully and it was covered with reed and raw skins for transportation. It was pulled in a carriage with forty-two wheels and had ropes attached to each wheel, with 200 men pulling each rope. So the next time you see it, do spare a thought for the labour of these men! Further, Hasan states:

> … orders were issued to commanding the attendance of all the people in the neighbourhood, and all soldiers, both horse and foot. They were ordered to bring instruments and materials suitable for the work. Directions were issued for bringing parcels of the cotton of the silk cotton tree. Quantities of this silk cotton were placed around the column, and when the earth at its base was removed, it fell gently over on the bed prepared for it. The cotton was then removed by degrees and after some days the pillar lay safe on the ground… The pillar was then encased from top to bottom in reeds and raw skins, so that no damage might accrue to it. The felling and transporting of the pillar was accomplished with the help of divine inspiration, in accordance with human understanding… every detail of the work including the tying of ropes and the construction of masonry piers; pulling ropes in all directions and balancing the pillar with their help; the employment of elephants for dragging the pillar, and following on their failure the employment of

> longer ropes with 20,000 men and their success in carrying the pillar to the banks of the Jamna; then arranging well balanced boats for the pillar, loading the pillar on the boats and floating the same; its journey to Firozabad (Delhi); the making of all the arrangements over again for removing the pillar and carrying it in front of the Jum'ah Mosque, there constructing a large building, raising and placing the pillar thereon with the help of pulleys etc., and re-erecting the pillar according to the laws of wisdom – a gift of the most exalted God…

The Sultan came to greet it when it entered Delhi, after which it was transferred to a boat capable of carrying 2000 maunds (approx 74,700 kg) and brought via the Yamuna.

> An account of the Raising of the Obelisk
>
> When the pillar was brought to the palace, a building was commenced for its reception, near the Jámi Masjid, and the most skilful architects and workmen were employed. It was constructed of stone and chúnam, and consisted of several stages or steps (poshish). When a step was finished the column was raised on to it, another step was then built and the pillar was again raised, and so on in succession until it reached the intended height. On arriving at this stage, other contrivances had to be devised to place it in an erect position. Ropes of great thickness were obtained, and windlasses were placed on each of the six stages of the base. The ends of the ropes were fastened to the top of the pillar, and the other ends passed over the windlasses, which were firmly secured with many fastenings. The wheels were then turned, and the column was raised about half a gaz. Logs of wood and bags of cotton were then placed under it to prevent its sinking again. In this way, by degrees,

> and in the course of several days, the column was raised to the perpendicular. Large beams were then placed round it as shores, until quite a cage of scaffolding was formed. It was thus secured in an upright position, straight as an arrow, without the smallest deviation from the perpendicular. The square stone, before spoken of, was placed under the pillar. After it was raised, some ornamental friezes of black and white stone were placed round its two capitals (do sar-i án), and over these there was raised a gilded copper cupola, called in Hindí kalas.
>
> *Shams Siraj Afif in Tarikh e Firoz Shahi*

The pillar had a gilded bronze cupola but that disappeared somewhere in the seventeenth century. The last documented reference is by William Finch in 1611. The pillar was referred to as *Minar e Zareen* or Golden Pillar because of the golden glow from the polished sandstone. However, that would be then; today it is called the 'Laat Waale Baba' as, according to popular belief, the chief of the jinns residing in the fort stays in the pillar!

How did jinns suddenly populate this abandoned city? None of the old texts, whether it's Sir Syed's *Asar-us-Sanadid* or Maulvi Zafar Hasan's *Monuments of Delhi,* mention it; yet, today to talk of Kotla is to talk of jinns.

Anand Vivek Taneja spent many years researching the city of jinn-saints and has described it in his book *Jinneology.* He writes that a black marketeer-turned-healer named Laddu Shah was the first to bring jinns into prominence. Taneja, who met Laddu Shah's son, describes how the jinns became extremely fond of Shah, who used to play a wind instrument near Ashoka's pillar, and started granting his wishes when he interceded for people. The dispossessed, disenchanted and those unhopeful of justice in the real world started coming here to the babas (jinn-saints) for justice.

Today, the cells and rooms under the mosque and the pillar are full of letters and petitions to the jinns or with diyas and flowers after the fulfilment of wishes.

There are very few visitors here except on Thursdays, when entry is free after 2 p.m. as people come to pray, make supplications to the jinns or make good on their pledges after the fulfilment of their wishes by distributing biryani and sweets.

As per Islam, jinns were created before man from smokeless fire. In fact, when Iblees, the chief jinn, was asked to prostrate in front of Adam, he refused on the grounds that he, originating from fire, was superior to Adam, who was made from clay. This led to his fall from grace and turned him into the accursed Satan.

Jinn is a plural noun in Arabic, literally meaning 'hidden from sight', and it derives from Arabic root *j-n-n* (pronounced: jinn) meaning 'to hide' or 'be hidden'.

As in human race, there are good and bad jinns. The word 'genie' comes from the Arabic 'jinn' and, as per folklore, has great powers to grant wishes. The village my ancestors come from was established by Jalaluddin Khilji and has a mosque dating back to the era. I have grown up hearing stories of jinn mamus from my grandmother and other relatives. We even have a jinn waali masjid there and, of course, many tales.

A conversation with the imam and his friend reinforced the idea of the benevolent jinns. According to him, every masjid has jinns; they guard the citadel and, in fact, Delhi. I'd like to believe that as long as jinns live in Delhi, no harm can come to it!

Dargah Saiyyed Badruddin Samarqandi

Man tu shudam tu man shudi, Man tan shudam tu jaan shudi.
Taa kas na goyad baad azeen, Man deegaram tu deegari
I have become you and you have become me. I have become the body and you have become the soul
So that no one can say I am different from you and you are different from me

Hazrat Amir Khusrau

Dargah Saiyyed Badruddin Samarqandi

Sheikh Saiyyed Badruddin Samarqandi was the disciple and successor to the Khalifa of Sheikh Saifuddin. He came from Bukhara to India and settled in a corner near Firoz Shah Kotla to enjoy Hazrat Nizamuddin Auliya's company. He was one of his followers and would often go to Hazrat Nizamuddin's *khanqah* to enjoy the *sema mehfils* held there.

The saint died in 1297 AD. His importance can be gauged from the fact that when Firoz Shah built his Ḳotla, he diverted the walls to accommodate his tomb. It can be seen from the road under the walls of the Kotla and, though it is not so popular today, it was once a centre for his devotees. The tiled grave stands on a platform and there are other graves around it.

Kalan Masjid

Saintliness is not to be purchased in shops
nor is it to be had for wandering
nor in cupboards
nor in deserts
nor in forests

Sant Tukaram[34]

This mosque stands near Turkman Gate, within the walls of Shahjahanabad, but I have included it here as it was also included within the area of Firozabad. The word 'kalan' means 'great', but the word has been corrupted and the building is sometimes called the Kali Masjid or Black Mosque.

It was built in 1387 and has the same style as that of the Khirki Masjid. It has a single open court and the special feature of the Tughlaq period, the sloping walls, which are so beautifully done, are called *salami deewar* (bending to pay respect) in Urdu. The tapering towers and massive columns of quartzite give it a very majestic appearance.

As in other Tughlaq buildings, this mosque was built for stability and strength, not beauty, and this can be seen from the rough nature of the arches and stones. The mortar used by these artisans was of an extremely superior quality to have lasted for so many centuries. It was built on a high plinth of 28 feet and the lower storey had rooms which were leased out to shops. There were two rooms under the minarets inside the stairs, which had a path to the main mosque; I doubt they exist today. A painting by Sita Ram in 1822 shows

Kalan Masjid, Shahjahanabad

a picnic of Lady Hastings in the open ground in front of it. Today, there is no place for anything as buildings crowd in from every side.

After I climbed the twenty-nine steps to the mosque and entered it, I was struck by the serenity and sense of peace there. There's a *hauz* with a fountain for *wuzu* in the courtyard and the aisles of the mosque are reflected in it, adding to its beauty. The mosque is 148 feet long and 120 feet wide with thick walls. From the second level to the roof, it is 38 feet in height. It has stone lintels instead of arches.

Basheeruddin Ahmad talks of thirty-three windows covered with red sandstone screens similar to Khirki Masjid but he adds that some have been closed with ordinary stones. I don't remember seeing any so I presume all have closed down with the passing of time. There are fifteen low domes over the mosque proper, arranged in three rows, and the same number covers the arcades; all are true horseshoe arches, which were prevalent before the bulbous dome came into fashion in the time of Shah Jahan.

It was known as Kali Masjid because of the black layer of dirt and soot that had accumulated on it but it's now a functioning mosque under the Delhi Waqf Board and has been repainted a bright green and white, reclaiming its original name of Kalan Masjid.

Tomb of Sultan Raziya

For several months, her face was veiled
— her sword's ray flashed, lightning-like, from behind the screen.
Since the sword remained in the sheath,
many rebellions were left unchecked.
With a royal blow, she tore away the veil;
she showed her face's sun from behind the screen.
The [lioness] showed so much force
that brave men bent low before her

Hazrat Amir Khusrau

Tomb of Sultan Raziya

If there is one woman from the medieval ages who fits the portrait of a romantic and tragic hero it is Raziya al-Din, who took the title of Sultan Jalalat -ud-din Raziya after ascending the throne of the Delhi Sultanate.

Coins were struck in the name of Sultánu-l 'azam Jalálatu-d dunyá wau-d dín Malikatu-l bint Altamshu-s Sultán Mihrat Amíru-l muminín, the great Sultán, the glory of the world and the Faith, the Queen, the daughter of the Sultán Altamsh, the beloved of the Commander of the Faithful.

Her father was Sultan Iltutmish, the third and most famous Mamluk ruler of the Delhi Sultanate. Sultan Raziya was born of Iltutmish's favourite wife, Terken Khatoon, the daughter of Sultan Qutbuddin Aibak.

Sultan Iltutmish's eldest and most capable son was Nasiruddin Mahmud, whom he had groomed as his successor. Unfortunately he was killed in a battle in Lakhnauti, Bengal where he was the governor in 1229, and his remaining brothers were considered incapable of becoming the Sultan by the father. Sultan Iltutmish had trained Sultan Raziya in politics and warfare from childhood and she was his favoured child, whom he appointed as his successor.

Minhaj us Siraj, a contemporary historian, reports that when the nobles protested, Sultan Iltutmish replied, 'engrossed in the pleasures of youth, and none of them possesses the capability of managing the affairs of the country,' whereas Raziya, his daughter, was the most worthy, as would be proven after his death.

This was a radical step for those days when women were confined to the harem alone. But Sultan Iltutmish, a far-sighted visionary, had not taken into account the aversion that the nobles had of being ruled by a woman. During the Mamluk reign, there was a band of powerful *chihilgani* (noblemen) who had removed Aram Shah, Sultan Qutbuddin Aibak's son, and put Sultan Iltutmish on the throne.

These nobles put Ruknuddin Firoz (April 1236–October 1236), his younger son, on the throne. Ruknuddin was a young man given to the pursuit of pleasure and the reigns of the kingdom were in the hand of his mother Shah Turkan, a vicious and ambitious lady. One of her first steps was to try and isolate Raziya from the day-to-day work of the kingdom. She also had Raziya's youngest brother, Muizuddin, murdered. She used her newfound status to settle old scores and attempted to have Raziya murdered too. This led to an uproar and taking advantage of Ruknuddin's absence, who had gone out of Delhi for a battle, backed by the army, Raziya went to Jami Masjid in Delhi (Quwatul Islam Masjid in the Qutub).

Khwaja Abdullah Malik Isami in his *Futuhas Salatin* (1349–50) wrote that she dressed herself in the garment worn by the aggrieved, showed herself to the people assembled for the Friday prayers and, in the name of her father, appealed for help against the intrigues of Shah Turkan. Her sight and her powerful words profoundly affected the people assembled there, leading to another radical step: an agreement between Sultan Raziya and the people of Delhi to the following effect: 'She was to be given a chance to prove her abilities and, if she did not prove better than men, her head was to be struck off.' By the time her brother came back to the city, Sultan Raziya's enthronement was complete and Shah Turkan had been thrown into prison. Both mother and son were executed on 9 November 1236.

This step, along with Sultan Iltutmish's decision in naming Raziya as his successor, gives an indication about the minds of the Turkish nobility and common men of that era. They were capable of taking such a bold step.

However, the nobles did not like her appreciation and dependence on her father's slave and her mentor, Malik Yaqut. He was not a Turk but an Abysinnian and that was considered a breach in the defences of the *chihilgani* slaves. They eventually outmanoeuvred her and when she rode out to quell the rebellion of Malik Altuniya, she was captured by him and imprisoned in the fort of Bathinda. Malik Yaqut had already been killed in the battle against Altuniya. Later, Sultan Raziya married Altuniya and rode out with him to fight her brother. She was killed in the battle.

Her simple grave lies near Turkman Gate in Bulbulikhana near Bhojila Pahari. It is known locally as Rajji Shajji ki Qabr. The other grave is said to be of her sister, Shazia. She was a devotee of Shah Turkman Bayabani, a thirteenth-century saint, and the place where she is buried is said to be his *khanqah*, his hospice. The *mutawalli* of Shah Turkman's dargah, Maulana Khalid Mirza, told me that she had died in his lifetime and he had her buried there.

According to Sir Syed, Sultan Raziya's grave was built by her brother and successor, Muizuddin Bahram Shah.

The lanes leading to her tomb are confusing and one has to ask for directions at Bhojila Pahari. There is an ASI board which leads into Bulbulikhana. At the end of some narrow, dingy lanes is another stone sign by ASI, which announces the last resting place of south Asia's first female monarch.

Khaamosh pattharo'n ne sunaayi woh daastan
Lamho'n mein jaane kitni sadi ji liye hain hum
What the stories these silent stones told me
I don't know how many ages I lived through

Shifa Kajgaonvi

There are claims that this is not Sultan Raziya's tomb. Places as far as Tonk in Rajasthan and Kaithal in Haryana assert that her tomb is there.

But evidence for her grave being in Bulbulikhana comes from the court historian of Sultan Firoz Shah (1309–1388), Shams Siraj Afif who wrote *Tarikh e Firozshahi* (History of India during the reign 1351–1388). He describes the building of the new city of Firozabad, known as Firoz Shah Kotla today, and details the eighteen villages and lands that were bought by the Sultan for its construction.

> The Sultán having selected a site at the village of Gáwín, on the banks of the Jumna, founded the city of Fíroz-ábád, before he went to Lakhnautí the second time. Here he commenced a palace, [...]and the nobles of his court having also obtained [giriftand] houses there, a new town sprang up, five kos distant from Dehlí. Eighteen places were included in this town, the kasba of Indarpat, the saráí of Shaikh Malik Yár Parán, the saráí of Shaikh Abu Bakr Túsí, the village of Gáwín, the land of Khetwára, the land of Lahráwat, the land of Andháwalí, the land of the saráí of Malika, the land of the tomb of Sultán Raziya, the land of Bhárí, the land of Mahrola, and the land of Sultánpur. So many buildings were erected that from the kasba of Indarpat to the Kúshk-i shikár, five kos apart, all the land was occupied.

Even today, land records are considered an authentic source of information and Afif wrote his book not too long after Sultan Raziya's death. Perhaps the most surprising and detailed account is that of Ibn Battuta in *Travels of Ibn Battuta* (1304–1368); its credibility is questioned by historians.

> When Ruknu-d dín had been killed, the soldiers agreed to place his sister, Raziya, on the throne. They proclaimed her Sovereign, and she reigned with absolute authority for four

years. She rode on horseback as men ride, armed with a bow and quiver, and surrounded with courtiers. She did not veil her face. She was eventually suspected of an intimacy with one of her slaves, an Abyssinian by birth, and the people resolved upon deposing her and giving her a husband. So she was deposed and married to one of her relations, and her brother, Násiru-d dín, obtained the supreme power.

After the deposition of Raziya, her younger brother, Násiru-d dín, ascended the throne, and for some time exercised royal authority. But Raziya and her husband revolted against him, mounted their horses, and, gathering round them their slaves and such disaffected persons as were willing to join them, they prepared to give battle. Násiru-d dín came out of Dehli with his slave and lieutenant Ghiyásu-d dín Balban, who became ruler of the kingdom after him. The opposing forces met, and Raziya was defeated and obliged to fly. Pressed by hunger and overcome with fatigue, she addressed herself to a man engaged in cultivating the ground and begged for food. He gave her a bit of bread, which she devoured, and then she was overpowered by sleep. She was dressed in the garments of a man; but when the peasant looked at her as she slept, he perceived under her upper garment a tunic trimmed with gold and pearls. Seeing she was a woman he killed her, stripped her of her valuables, drove away her horse, and buried her corpse in his field. He then carried some of her garments to the market for sale. The dealers suspected him, and took him before the magistrate, who caused him to be beaten. The wretch then confessed that he had killed Raziya, and told his guards where he had buried her. They exhumed her body, washed it, and, wrapping it in a shroud, buried it again in the same place. A small shrine was erected over her grave, which is visited by pilgrims, and is considered a place of sanctity. It is situated on the banks of the Jumna, about a parasang from Dehli.

Ferishta, who wrote at a much later date than the rest, makes the only reference to Kathihal. It is therefore possible that as it was during his time that there was a creative renaissance and his version was accepted by the historians who followed him.

Tonk does not figure anywhere in any narrative of any medieval historian. Yaqut had died when Sultan Raziya married Altunia and she came back to Delhi to fight her brother and was killed, so there is no question of both of them being buried together. These lurid tales of their love are recent additions as they seemed the only way to explain looking up to him for guidance and support. He was probably her mentor and father figure.

Mehndiya'n

Hasti apni habaab ki si hai,
Yeh numaaish saraab ki si hai
My life is like a bubble
This world seems a mirage

Mir Taqi Mir

This was an iconic monument and has graced the cover of many a book on medieval Delhi monuments. It no longer exists but I am describing it here for reference as not much is known about it. It was between Turkman and Delhi Darwaza, located inside Firozabad, the city built by Sultan Firoz Shah, and only its ruins existed in the early twentieth century. It was a circular tower and measured 118 feet × 88 feet built on a 12 feet high plinth. It had arched entrances in the lower portion with four *burjis* on each of the four sides and one in the centre.

There is no authentic proof of the name of the builder but as per legend, a nawab saheb who had great faith in Syed Abdul Qadir Jilani, Ghaus-ul-Azam, built it in 1354 AD. In Sufi traditions, particularly in India, *urs* celebrations are held to commemorate the death anniversaries of sufi saints. Mehndiya'n was for celebrating the *urs* of Syed Abdul Qadir Jilani. The custom was to make bamboo structures, cover it with bright coloured paper and light lamps on it. This was called *menhdi*.

This nawab saheb also used to take out a *menhdi*. When he became rich and in a position to do something for his saint, he got this built in the same shape as the bamboo *menhdi*. He would illuminate this building and give charity on the day of the ceremony. Nothing else is known about him, though.

This monument became famous as Kushk e Mehndiya'n. It was immortalized by the Daniells (William and Thomas) in watercolour and it is one of the most iconic paintings of medieval India. The Maulana Azad Medical College now stands on this location.

Dargah of Sheikh Waliullah

Secretly we spoke,
that wise one and me.
I said, Tell me the secrets of the world.
He said, Shh... Let silence
Tell you the secrets of the world

Mevlana Rumi[35]

Near the Mehdiya'n is a medieval graveyard, which is now known as Mehndiya'n. The relatives of Shah Abdul Aziz were buried here. Therefore, the shrines of Janab Maulana Shah Waliullah saheb, Maulana Shah Abdul Aziz saheb, Maulana Rafi-ud-din saheb and Maulvi Abdul Quddus saheb Qudd-us-Allah are here. It is well looked after and a small room has been built over the grave of the saint.

Dargah of Sheikh Waliullah

Grave of Momin Khan Momin

Momin Khan Momin is one of the greats of Urdu poetry. A contemporary of Mirza Ghalib, it is said that Mirza Ghalib offered his entire *diwan* (collection of poems) in exchange for one verse:

> *Tum mere paas hote ho goya*
> *Jab koi doosra nahin hota*
> *Its as if you are with me*
> *When no one else is*

He was born into a family of hakims (physicians) and he himself was a practising hakim. He also took much interest in astrology.

A religious man, he was buried in the compound of the Sufi saint, Shah Waliullah (1703–1762). He was an Islamic scholar, reformer and founder of modern Islamic thought who attempted to reassess Islamic theology in the

Grave of Momin Khan Momin

light of modern changes. The area where Shah Waliullah is buried was called Mehndiya'n and this was part of the Qabristan e Mehndiya'n.

Dargah of Mir Dard

Shamaa ki maanind ham is bazm mein
chashm-nam aaye the daaman-tar chale
Like a candle to this gathering
I came with wet eyes, and left with a damp hem

Khwaja Mir Dard

Khwaja Mir Dard (1721–1785), along with Mir Taqi Mir and Mirza Sauda, is considered one of the three major poets of the Delhi school. Mir Taqi Mir, perhaps the greatest of all the Urdu poets as acknowledged by Mirza Ghalib, was a poet who wrote about love and pathos. Mirza Sauda is remembered for

Dargah of Mir Dard

his satire and panegyric. Khwaja Mir Dard, a Sufi saint of the Naqshbandi Majdudi silsila, was a mystic poet. His greatness lay in translating mysticism into verse. Sample this:

Tujhi ko jo yaan jalwa farma na dekha
Baraabar hai duniya ko dekha na dekha
If I did not see the display of your splendour
It matters little whether I saw the world or not

I went in search of his mazar and, though many people were unaware of its whereabouts, an old man told me it was next to Zakir Hussain College.

The entrance to Khwaja Mir Dard Basti, an urban slum (adjacent to Zakir Hussain College) that has been named in the poet's honour, houses the tomb. One can enter it either from here or walk a little further and enter the *basti* from the lane near a petrol pump after the college. None of the roads are clean. After walking for ten minutes and some false starts – because there is a mosque named after him too – I reached his mazar. It's a rundown uncared for and depressing circular building made of bricks with a tin roof.

There are thirteen graves inside with the poet's grave on the left corner. These include Mir Dard's grandson, Khwaja Nasir Wazir Andaleeb, and his younger brother Khwaja Mohammad Mir Asar. The headstone is worn out and I had a tough time deciphering his name. The peeling paint and the dirty graves bear mute testimony to our neglect of our icons. A forlorn diya sits in one corner.

Khafa ho ke ai 'Dard' mar to chalaa tuu
kahan tak gham apna chhupata rahega
O Dard, you have reached death's door by concealing your emotions
Till when will you hide your sorrows

Khwaja Mir Dard

This is the tomb of someone who is considered the greatest mystic poet of Urdu. Maybe his pen name, Dard (sorrow/pain), was prophetic. I certainly was very pained. Once upon a time, it was in a small orchard named after the poet.

Dargah Khwaja Baqi Billah

If you keep seeking the jewel of understanding,
then you are a mine of understanding in the making.
If you live to reach the Essence one day,
then your life itself is an expression of the Essence.
Know that in the final analysis you are that
which you search for

Abu Said Abil Kheir[36]

Dargah Khwaja Baqi Billah

Hazrat Baqi Billah was the sufi saint responsible for establishing the Naqshbandi silsila in India. The son of Qazi Abdul Salam Khilgi Samarqandi Qureishi, a famous scholar and saint of Kabul, Razi-ud-Din Mohammad Baqi was born in Kabul in 971 AH or 1563 AD. He was popularly known as Baqi Billah. Spiritual from birth, he became inclined towards Sufism and travelled through central Asia to India. He saw Khawaja Baha-ud-Din Naqshband, bestowing spiritual favours on him. On his way to Mavara-ur-Nahr, he dreamt that Hazrat Khawaja Amkangi was calling him and anxiously waiting for him, so he went to see him at his abode and stayed there for three days. Khawaja Amkangi blessed him with his Khilafat (spiritual caliphate) and said: 'Go to India because this Order [Naqshbandia silsila] will be established there by you.'

Though he knew it was a difficult task, he set out for Delhi to fulfil it. He stayed in Qila Firozabad or Firoz Shah Kotla and would sweep the graveyard there; the area which now falls in Maulana Azad Medical College. He established and strengthened the Naqshbandi silsila in India. He performed innumerous miracles. He believed in minimalism, be it speaking, eating or sleeping. At night he would complete reading the Quran twice over. He passed away at the age of forty in 1603 AD. His dargah was built in the same year to the west of Sadar Bazar. There is a beautiful qasida, a panegyric, written in his praise on the wall behind his grave. It is a simple shrine, small in size next to a mosque, but has an extremely spiritual ambience and is a place rich in blessings.

The entrance to his dargah is called Buland Darwaza and leads one into a graveyard. In the twentieth century, this was the largest and the most sought after graveyard as it was considered a blessing to be buried near the saint.

The sons of Emperor Bahadur Shah, who were killed by Captain Hodson after the fall of Delhi into British hands in 1857, are also said to be buried here.

The atmosphere of the graveyard is very 'alive' with squeals and shouts from children playing amongst the graves.

Children who live near graveyards grow up with a nonchalance about death, I feel. For them life goes on amidst death. These children of the family living here were playing, fighting and having fun as I stood and watched them.

One enters an extremely beautiful and tranquil mosque, looked after by Janab Salamat Ullah Naqshbandi, a direct descendant of Hazrat Baqi Billah and the *mujavir* (caretaker) of the dargah. Old and frail, Pir Saheb, as he is known, looked very spiritual and serene and I was very impressed by his personality. Though he was preparing for namaz, he kindly took me around and patiently answered my questions; he even posed for photographs.

The mosque is beautiful and well maintained. There are no crowds of supplicants or beggars and it is a place of solitude and meditation.

According to Hazrat Khwaja Baqi Billah, *tavakkal* (trust in Allah) does not mean that a person should not earn his living and become idle as that is an act of disobedience to Allah. Everyone should earn their living in any manner they can and believe that only Allah is the Sustainer. He did not approve of saints living the life of hermits and renouncing the world. According to him, work is just like a source, mediation or an intercessor and worldly struggle strengthens one's spirit.

He passed away on 29 November 1603. His tomb is in a small green building just outside the mosque and very well kept. It is said that one night, Hazrat Baqi Billah, after having offered his Tahajjud prayers, came to his bed to rest. To his great surprise, he saw a cat crouching on his bed. The kind-hearted Khwaja Baqi Billah did not disturb the cat but quietly sat down on the floor and passed the rest of the night in the chilly winter, whereas the cat slept soundly till morning.

This dargah is on Qutab Road, Singara Chowk, near Sadar Bazar Area.

Qadam Sharif

A mystic is one
who passes away –
He abides in the essence
of that which is Real.
Such a person is pure,
clear wine without dregs.
Now whole, he displays
the Most Beautiful Names.

Binavi Badakshani[37]

After reading Shamsur Rahman Farooqi's *The Mirror of Beauty*, I was very intrigued by a description of a popular and revered shrine called Qadam Sharif. Having spent a lot of time in Delhi, I was surprised that I had never heard of this shrine and was determined to find out where it was and go there. In the book, when misfortune strikes Nawab Mirza Shamsuddin Ahmed Khan of Firozepur Jhirka, Wazir Khanum makes a trip to the shrine. The author describes it as a beautiful and busy place with supplicants and mendicants both going about their business. In fact, the impression I got was of a 'mela', the kind one sees on *urs* days in the dargahs.

I set off, armed with directions from various guidebooks, but the shrine is impossible to find unless someone knowledgeable guides you.

I found my guide in the form of a young boy I noticed in the dargah of Khwaja Baqi Billah and then began a heartbreaking journey. The road to it, called Nabi Kareem Road, went through the narrow bylanes and galis of Paharganj and we entered the dargah through what must once have been a splendid entrance. Today it is a dilapidated structure used as a dumping ground.

Once these streets must have echoed with the sounds of:

'Ba Adab, baa mulaihzaa hoshiyar!
Sultan e Aala tashreef laa rahe hain!'
Stand at attention, pay respects, The Sultan approaches.

Today there is no one to help you negotiate your way around this desolate place. I found children playing outside (cricket on the graves seemed fun!) who called the *mutawalli* from his house. There are three iron doors at the entrance of the dargah which are normally shut and opened only on request. The *mutawalli* told me this was to prevent goats from straying inside and littering the place. Qadam Sharif is the imprint on a marble slab of the Prophet Mohammad (pbuh) which was acquired by Firoz Shah Tughlaq.

Metcalfe writes:

> The Tradition is that in the time of the Emperor Firoz Shah about five centuries ago, a celebrated Devotee and a Disciple of the Emperor's was deputed to Mecca (to which all true Mohummudans are bound to make one Pilgrimage, if they hope for Salvation) to obtain from the Caliph of that place a Khillut or Dress of Honor. The Boon was granted, and in addition as a mark of high consideration the Slab in question was also consigned to the care of the Devotee. It was brought to Dehly. The Emperor and all his Nobles proceeded to a distance of 15 miles from the city to do honor to this precious relic. It was escorted with much pomp and finally deposited by order of the emperor in the royal treasury.

The stone with the Prophet's footprint was brought from Mecca by Makhdum Jahanian Jahan, the spiritual guide of the Sultan.

Once Firoz Shah asked his favourite son, Fateh Khan, what he would like from the imperial treasury. The young prince asked for the Qadam Sharif. The Sultan refused but promised that it would be buried with whoever between them died first.

Unfortunately, the prince died first (1374 AD) and, as per his promise the Sultan erected this tomb and had the precious slab kept on his son's grave.

The tomb is inside a high building with a unique shape. Inside a huge hall lies the grave of the unfortunate prince. There was a marble basin measuring 9 feet × 4.5 feet × 1.5 feet placed on the grave. On the location of the heart, the Qadam Sharif itself was kept inside this tank. This tank used to be kept filled with water, milk and flowers. No traces of it remain.

People who came here for *ziarat* of the Qadam Sharif would take this liquid as a *tabarruk* (holy offering) and recite the following verse:

Ai Khizr e dil isko peeye se nijaat hai
Paani Qadam Sharif ka aab e hayat hai
O immortal heart, a sip of this leads to salvation
The water of Qadam Sharif is no less than aab e hayat
[Water of a sacred spring in Mecca called Zamzam]

It is now with the *khadim*, who keeps it in his house for safekeeping. On my request he brought it out.

Sultan Bhai as he is known, is the *mutawalli* of the dargah and it was from him I heard of the sad tale of the degeneration of this beautiful shrine. According to him, hordes of refugees took shelter in and around the place during Partition and later settled down. The encroachments are still visible.

Qila Qadam Sharif (Courtesy: ASI archives)

Since it was the grave of his favourite son, the Sultan built it with a lot of care, love and sadness. There was a madrasa attached to it and a well or tank filled with *aab e zam zam* (water from the holy spring in Mecca). I didn't find traces of it in the premises.

Even today it is called the Qila Qadam Sharif because of the fortified walls and gates the Sultan built. There are domes in the corners of the dargah with corridors running from it, each containing graves.

It became the graveyard of many luminaries and it was only in the late nineteenth century that the British stopped burials there and in other holy sites within the city. Opposite the steps, which lead up to the raised platform of the enclosure, is the grave of Nawab Mirza Shamsuddin Ahmed Khan of Firozepur Jhirka, hanged for participation in the murder of William Fraser in 1835.

At Qadam Sharif, the annual *urs* is held on Barawafat, the Holy Prophet's (pbuh) birthday. On that day, the slab with the imprint of his foot is immersed in water and offered to devotees as *tabarruk*.

I end with a description from *Muraqqa e Delhi* written by Dargah Quli Khan, a young visitor who came to Delhi from the Deccan in 1737–41 AD.

He wrote: 'Every Thursday the courtyard of the Dargah is so full of visitors that it is difficult even to approach the place and touch it. Pilgrims and ascetics come from countries far and near to seek fulfilment of their wishes.'

He goes on to rather disapprovingly describe the behaviour and demeanour of the crowds, where there are beautiful women carrying porcelain bottles of perfumes, uncontrollable crowds and ecstatic singers, with the *mehfil* becoming gay and boisterous.

Alas, today I did not find the spiritual solace I went looking for and came back with a heavy heart at the general air of neglect which hangs in the tragically rundown place.

A masjid called Masjid Chauraha Qadam Sharif had been built near this dargah, in the same style as Kalan Masjid, but it has been swallowed inside some residential complex as I found no traces of it anywhere nearby.

The Dargah was called Qila Qadam Sharif as it was built in the style of a fort with proper fortified walls, gateways and bastions. Today it is limited to a small area.

Tuti e Hind Sheikh Mohammad Ibrahim Zauq ka Mazar

Laayi hayaat aaye, qazaa le chalii chale
na apni khushii aaye, na apni khushii chale
Life brought me, death took me away
I neither came of my free will, nor did happiness have a say

Zauq

Sheikh Ibrahim Zauq was the poet laureate and ustad of the Mughal Emperor Bahadur Shah Zafar.

Sheikh Ibrahim was born on 11 Zil-Hajj 1204 AH (1789 AD). His father was an ordinary soldier with straitened circumstances but he ensured

that his son got a good education under Hafiz Ghulam Rasool Shauq, who ran a madrasa in their neighbourhood. Hafiz Ghulam Rasool Shauq was a poet and there were many discussions on poetry in his house. The effect of this environment on the young Ibrahim was the awakening of a desire to write and he started taking guidance from Hafiz ji, who suggested the *takhallus* of Zauq for him. Later on, he became the student of Shah Naseer and started showing him his ghazals. He also started participating in mushairas. He would often get disheartened because of his modest circumstances and lack of patronage. One day he recited a ghazal based on a ghazal of the famous Urdu satirist Sauda and took it to Shah Naseer. The latter was offended that his student had the effrontery to write a ghazal based on the work of such a famous poet and threw it away. He came back even more disheartened.

There was a mushaira to be held at the same time where he wanted to recite this ghazal. However, as a master poet had not corrected or improved it, he was apprehensive. Lost in thought, he reached the Jama Masjid in Shahjahanabad where he met Mir Kallu Haqeer, a poet he had met in mushairas. On being asked, Sheikh Ibrahim described his state of mind and read out the ghazal. Mir Kallu Haqeer encouraged him to read it and not worry about critics.

Thus he read the ghazal, which was highly appreciated, and received much needed encouragement. Soon, he started reading his uncorrected ghazals in mushairas and became very famous.

Emperor Bahadur Shah Zafar was a poet and a connoisseur of poetry. When he was the heir to the throne, one of his trusted nobles, Mir Kazim Hussain Beqarar, also a poet, introduced him to Zauq, who recited one of his ghazals for him.

Since at that time, Shah Naseer, who had been the ustad of the prince, had gone to the Deccan, Zauq stepped into that space. The first ghazal of the prince that he improved met with his approval and so it became a regular affair. He was appointed at Rs 4 a month as the ustad of the Prince. Though this was a mere pittance, Zauq accepted the post. Later, he read a qasida in praise of Emperor Akbar Shah II in light of which he was rewarded with the title of *Khaqani e Hind*. He was nineteen years old at the time. He continued to be the poet laureate under Emperor Bahadur Shah Zafar and his salary was raised to Rs 100. He passed away in 1854 after seventeen days of an illness. He said this verse a few hours before his death:

Kahte hain aaj Zauq jahan se guzar gaya
Kya khoob aadmi tha Khuda maghferat kare
They say that Zauq has passed away from this world
What a man he was! May God forgive him his sins[38]

I will start with a description of Zauq's grave from Basheeruddin Ahmad's book and then come to present day.

There was a famous nineteenth and twentieth century graveyard near Qadam Sharif known as Kallu ka Takiya (*takiya* meant the dwelling place of a saint) with three trees – imli, peepal and neem – growing in the same spot. Next to it was a small enclosure, which was the last resting place of the Mughal poet laureate Sheikh Mohammad Ibrahim Zauq.

There was a tombstone at the head of the grave with the inscription:

Allah ho Akbar
Tuti e Hind Hazrat e Ustad Zauq ne
Li gulshan e jahan se jo bagh e jinaa'n ki raah
Saal e wafat jo koi pooche to ai Zafar
Kah 'Zauq jannati' za sar e bakshish e ilaah
God is Great
The poet laureate Hazrat e Ustad Zauq
Left this worldly garden for the heavenly one
If someone asks his year of death, O Zafar
Say 'Zauq is a dweller of Paradise' because of God's blessings

Bahadur Shah Zafar himself wrote this chronogram for his tomb out of respect and love for his teacher. There were a total eight graves inside the enclosure. Basheeruddin Ahmad lamented the state of the enclosure in 1919 itself and said that though he had such famous students, no one had bothered to come and look after it. If this state continues, it won't be surprising if all signs of the grave are obliterated.

Ahmad was prophetic because that indeed is what happened. A public lavatory was made on the spot at some point after 1947 for the refugees who had come to settle in Paharganj. This urinal was later removed on court orders, after many petitions by Urdu lovers.

Today an enclosure exists with a cenotaph in almost the same area. Since no one knows where the tombstone or the grave is, the enclosure is called *Nishaan e Zauq*.

VI

Dinpanah/ Shergarh

Purana Qila

Bagh e Bedil

Harkî raft az dîdah dâghe bar dîl-e mâ tâzah kard
dar zamîn-e narm naqsh pâ nomâyân meshawad
The one who is out of my sight, left a wound in my heart
The soft earth reflects the footprints

Mirza Bedil[39]

The great Persian poet Mirza Abdul Qadir Bedil was born in India in 1644 AD, during the reign of Emperor Shah Jahan, and died in 1720 AD when the Mughal empire was faltering under Emperor Mohammad Shah. Popularly known

Bagh e Bedil

as Bedil Dehlavi, he is a highly respected poet. He was born to an Uzbeki family from Turkestan that moved to India in the early seventeenth century.

All his poetry has been well-preserved, with his complete works consisting mainly of ghazals, *tarkib-bands*, a *tarjih-band* and *mu'ammas* (riddles). He also wrote four *masnavis*, the most important being *Irfaan* which he completed at the age of sixty-eight. He is a prominent poet of the Indian school of poetry in Persian literature, and both Mirza Ghalib and Allama Iqbal were influenced by his unique style. A result of the tolerant times of the later Mughals, he sided with the common man rather than the clergy.

Daryâ nakashî, agar nahangî nakunî
bar kooh natâzî, ar palangî nakunî
yak jur'a-e tust, qulzam-e kown wa makân
ai hawsêla-e khîyâl tangî nakunî
You cannot sip the ocean, if you cannot be like a whale
You cannot gallop up the mountain, if you cannot be like a tiger
the world's ocean becomes one gulp for you
O the patience of imagination, if you do not lose capacity[41]

By nature he was inclined towards Sufism and spent time with the Sufi saints of his time. He is considered a Sufi saint by many. He essentially believed that the world was eternal and in constant motion. He believed that all life was first mineral, then plant, and then animal. His tomb has been built near Pragati Maidan and is now well-maintained as a garden.

Today, the area is famous as Bagh e Bedil regarding which there's a controversy, dealt with below, again recounted by Janab Mohammad Misbah.

Regarding tomb of Mirza Abdul Qadir Bedil, Janab Mohammad Misbah sahab, Naib Muttawalli, whose family has been the caretaker of the place for at least 600 years. He said that as per history, Bedil lived in a haveli on the banks of the river Yamuna bought for him by Nawab Sharfuddin. He died there and was buried in a place chosen by him earlier in the haveli itself.

This is proven by Urdu texts from that and later eras. For example, *Nikat e Bedil* published by Attaullah.

'But this is not the original mazar. This is actually Dargah Hazrat Khwaja Nooruddin Malik Yaar e Parran,' said Abdul Misbah, According to him, Bedil had died in his haveli and six months later his Afghan followers took his body and buried it in Kabul.

Dr Abdul Ghani corroborates this in his book *Life and Works of Abdul Qadir Bedil*. He writes:

> '[Bedil] was down with typhoid fever towards the end of Muharram 1133 AH (Nov. 1720). After four or five days the fever disappeared, and, thinking that he had recovered, Bedil took a bath on the 2nd of Safar 1133 AH (December 3, 1720). On Wednesday the 3rd of Safar there was a relapse of fever, which remained for the whole of the night. Nawab Ghairat Khan Bahadur[40] ... was with him for the whole of the night. Sometimes Bedil swooned, and then came to himself. When he regained senses, he would burst into laughter involuntarily. The hopes of recovery waned at last, and at dawn the condition changed horribly. It was Thursday, 4th Safar 1133 AH (December 5, 1720) when six gharis had passed after sunrise, the Bedil's soul winged its way to Heaven. His sacred remains were buried in the courtyard of his house, on the bank of the river Jamna, at the place specified by himself.'[41]

Khushgo is said to have written the chronogram for the tomb:

Alas! Bedil concealed his face from this world!
That pure jewel sleeps under the earth
When Khushgo asked his intellect for the chronogram
It said 'Mirza Bedil departed from this world[42]

In 2006, when Emomali Rahmanov, the President of Tajikistan, visited India, he wanted to pay tribute to the poet, who is a major saint for Central Asians.

The present location was fixed upon by Khwaja Hasan Nizami who translated Dargah Quli Khan's book Muraqqa e Dehli from Persian. Since Bedil's tomb was mentioned in it but no one knew of its exact location he published a query in the magazine where the translation appeared. A Maulana Shah Sulaiman Sahib of Phulwari replied saying that the tomb was in front of the Old Fort and in the vicinity of the tomb of Hazrat Malik Nuruddin Yaar e Parran. Khwaja Hasan Nizami visited the site and though he didn't find any vestiges of the tomb he discovered the site. He requested Nizam Asif Jah VII for help and the latter sent 2,000 rupees and the tomb with a marble tombstone and low enclosure of bricks was built.

Dargah of Sheikh Nuruddin Malik Yaar Parra'n

Saudagiri nahin ye ibaadat Khuda ki hai
Ai be-khabar jaza ki tamanna bhi chod de
It's worship of the Almighty not some trade
Oh ignorant one, give up desires of return

Allama Iqbal

Khwaja Hazrat Nuruddin was a Sufi saint of the Qadri silsila. He was the disciple of Hazrat Sheikh Aizazuddin Daniyal Khilji. He came to India from Persia and decided to settle on the banks of the river Yamuna, in an area that belonged to Sheikh Abu Bakr Tusi, more popularly known as Matka Shah. Sheikh Toosi objected to the entry of someone whom he thought had come without permission and asked, 'How have you come here?'

According to Akbarul Akhyar, Khwaja Nuruddin replied, 'My Pir [spiritual guide] has sent me here.'

Sheikh Tusi asked, 'Do you have any proof of that?'

Khwaja Nuruddin covered himself with a cloth and within minutes came back with a letter from his Pir, showing the *sanad* to Sheikh Abu Bakr Tusi. The speed impressed Matka Shah, who said, 'You are Malik Yaar Parra'n.' (A king/friend on the wing). This is how he got the title of Malik Yaar Parra'n.

Sultan Balban, the reigning monarch, was very inclined towards the mendicants and saints who came to Delhi or were settled here. He immediately granted him permission and gifted him four villages for the expenses of the saint and feeding of the poor who would visit him.

Janab Mohammad Misbah whose family has been caretaker of the shrine for over 600 years told us this story.

Sheikh Malik Yaar Parra'n's shrine is on a 15 square feet platform, which is 5 feet high. The headstone of the grave translates as:

> Sheikh Nuruddin Malik Yaar Parra'n, may God purify his grave, was a great and venerable saint. Sultan-ul-Mashaikh was his contemporary and used to visit his tomb. On the 18th Jumada II of the year 680 AH (4 October, 1281 AD) he repaired to the holy word. (*Fida*)

Janab Mohammad Misbah saheb led us to Khwaja saheb's grave and prayed for us after offering the fatiha for the departed soul.

His advice: be constant in your prayers and faith. *Maangne waale ko sab kuch milta hai lekin maangne waale ko zabaan chahiye* (A supplicant will always have his prayers fulfilled, as long as he asks with pious intentions). It is said that fairies reside there.

Hazrat Sheikh Baba Abu Bakr Toosi's Mazaar

Hazrat Sheikh Baba Abu Bakr Tusi's Mazar/Matka Shah

> *Charha mansoor sooli par, jo wakif tha wohi dilbar*
> *Arey mullah janaza parh, mein jaanoon mera khuda jaaney*
> *Mansoor was hanged, only those who knew his love for God understood his total annihilation of himself in God's love*
> *O priests, recite his funeral prayers,*
> *It is between me and my God*
>
> *Hazrat Shah Niaz*

Chances are you have heard of Matka Peer for its famous biryani, which is supplied in marriages and functions, or like me, are fascinated by the *matkas* (earthern pots) hanging from trees every time you go to Pragati Maidan or Purana Qila. However, Matka Peer is, in fact, the shrine of a very famous Qalandari saint. It is situated on a hillock near Pragati Maidan under which the river Yamuna used to flow a few centuries ago.

The actual name of Matka Shah Peer is Sheikh Hazrat Abu Bakr Tusi Haideri Qalandari. But to his numerous devotees he is just known as Matka Peer. Hazrat Nizamuddin Auliya would often visit him in his khanqah and the two would have spiritual discussions. Originally this khanqah was spread over 20 bigha 8 katta land but only the area on which the shrine is located is now left with them. This khanqah was below the hillock and had a Jannati Darwaza (door of Paradise). All around the dargah you will see matkas, either hanging from trees or stacked around the shrine.

The shrine is now on a 10 metre-high hillock, approachable by steps. It is a very beautiful shrine of modern construction. Sixteen delicate pillars form engrailed arches and support a flat roof that houses the shrine. Mirror work decorates it from inside. A courtyard surrounds it and it is always full of visitors and qawwals.

An inscription on the outside wall gives details of the saint. He died in 1257 AD. According to legend, the saint who lived during the reign of Sultan Ghiyasuddin Balban, cured a man of an incurable disease by giving him a sip from his matka. On hearing news of this incident, Sultan Balban sent clay pots filled with mud and iron balls to the saint as an offering. The saint covered the pots; started praying and at the end of his prayers, the covers on the pots were lifted and the iron balls and mud were gone. The people around saw that it had roasted gram and jaggery in them.

Even today devotees whose wishes/mannat have been fulfilled offer matkas and jaggery and gram. It is a place which though next to a very busy road, is very calm and peaceful. There is no one asking the devotees for money or any other subscription. One can sit and pray in peace.

Qalandars are ascetic Sufi dervishes who may or may not be connected to a specific Sufi order. They are different from other saints and they have very strong feelings of love for God's creation.

Purana Qila

Success and failure? No known address.
This or that goes on, depending on the other.
And who can say if Milord Shao was happier
ruling a city, or sacked, his excellent melon patch?

T'ao Ch'ien[43]

This fort was built by Emperor Humayun for the sixth city of Delhi known as Dinpanah in 1533 AD. It is also known as Inderpat after the legendary kingdom of the Pandavas, Indraprastha. The ASI has not found any conclusive proof of such a place during excavations in 2014.

Emperor Humayun was defeated by Emperor Sher Shah Suri in 1540 AD before he could build much more than its walls and gateways. Emperor Sher Shah Suri had most of the buildings inside the area built during his reign and the similar styles of the time make it hard to distinguish which ruler built which portion of the walls. The *Humayun Namah* of Khond Amir refers to Dinpanah the asylum of religious scholars and saints. The place is known as Purana Qila, Qila e Kuhna or Old Fort today.

It is said Emperor Humayun chose an auspicious time in 1533 AD to start construction, offering namaz and laying a token brick for its foundation. The gates and walls was ready within ten months. Dinpanah had three darwazas and measured 3 furlongs (0.6035052 km) in length and 4 furlongs (0.8046736 km) in width. Two of these gates are now kept closed. There are three postern or wicket gates that open toward the river. There are seven lofty and magnificent bastions on the corners of the wall. There were two-storeyed apartments inside the city situated near the city walls. The walls were made of quartzite with strong battlements. These are now in ruins.

Till 1924, a village called Inderpat flourished inside the Purana Qila. Villagers were evacuated on the orders of the viceroy, Lord Curzon, in 1919. There used to be a cemetery honouring those killed in the first war of Indian independence in 1857.

Bara Darwaza or Main Gate

This is the main gate (as suggested by the name) and the one in use today. It is flanked by lofty octagonal bastions on each side, decorated with encaustic tiles. Remnants of these tiles are still visible. There were two small cupolas on top of these bastions, of which one has fallen. There is a row of *jharokhas* over the arch of the doorway.

Humayun's Gate

This is a magnificent three-storeyed darwaza similar to the other two gates. On both sides and the top of the gateway are engravings of a horse. It measures 60 feet by 10 feet. This site is not visited much, as it is mostly visible from afar.

Talaqi Gate

This lofty grey and red sandstone gate is known as the Talaqi Darwaza (or Forbidden Gateway). According to legend, it was said that if a king reentered this gateway having lost in battle, he would be divorced from his wives. When the king in this so-called legend died in battle, the gate was never opened. As there is no reference to the story in historical texts, we cannot verify this tale.

The darwaza has a high, central-arched door, and another arched window above it, with two *jharokhas* on either side. There is a small window in the centre above the arch. The gate is 50 feet high and 24 feet wide, with two magnificent bastions on either side. There is a band of marble above it which may have been for an inscription. There are three open pavilions on the roof of the gate. Inside the fort are beautiful semi circular steps leading down to the gate. The exterior is accessible only from the lake which surrounds the fort these days.

Masjid Qila e Kuhna

Ye imtiaz zaroori hai ab ibaadat mein
Vahi dua jo nazar kar rahi hai lab bhi kare'n
This distinction is necessary in worship
That the lips ask for what the gaze seeks

Abhishek Shukla

Abbas Khan Sarwani in his book *Tarikh e Sher Shani* and Abdullah in *Tarikh e Daudi* mentions the construction of this mosque by Emperor Sher Shah.

It measures 168 feet by 44.5 feet in size. It is 44 feet high from the floor to the roof, and 16 feet from the roof to top of the dome. It has five arched doorways with the central one being the tallest as 40 feet by 25 feet in size. There is a beautiful geometric design and Naskh and Tughra calligraphy on the doorway, with small Rajasthani *jharokha* on top of the arch. Inlay work has been done with white and black marble.

This doorway has two small minarets springing from supporting pilasters on either side. There are two more minarets at the edges of the roof, which are of the same size.

The side arches are also beautifully decorated with small *jharokhas* on top. There used to be three domes on the roof but only the central one remains today. It is crowned by a heavy lotus finial developed under the Lodis.

It also has five arched qibla mihrabs of great beauty. Each is different from the other and richly decorated with black and white marble and red sandstone, Quranic calligraphy and names of Allah inscribed on it. A marble pulpit that used to be here now no longer exists.

I find the pendentives supporting the mosques the most majestic and beautiful parts of this mosque. Stairways leading to the top are kept locked behind a grilled door now. The mosque is one of the finest specimens of Pathan architecture and continues the single aisle design of the Lodis that culminated under the Mughals.

Masjid Qila e Kuhna

Well and Hauz

There is a sixteen-sided tank attached to the mosque, the well next to which was built in 1907. According to the inscription beside it, the well was built by Siraj-ul-Millat-wa-deen, the Amir Habibullah Khan of Afghanistan, for the benefit of worshippers of the mosque, and to commemorate his visit here in January 1907.

According to Basheeruddin Ahmad, the *hauz* in front of the mosque is a latter-day construction and not part of the original mosque. It was built in 1919 when the fort was evacuated of villagers and landscaped.

The British built this concrete *hauz* measuring 61.4 feet in diameter and 4.10 feet deep. Water from the nearby Yamuna was pumped into it and used for watering the gardens.

Hammam

There are ruins of a hammam near the Sher Mandal. The hammam was an important part of Turkish and Mughal life.

Sher Mandal

Sada aish dauraan dikhaata nahin
Gaya waqt phir haath aata nahin
Time doesn't always present you with luxury
Time that has slipped away, never returns

Meer Hasan

Emperor Sher Shah constructed this in 1541 AD[44] as a 'Jahannuma' (or, 'reflecting the world'), naming it Sher Mandal. It is said this small palace could not be completed.

Sher Mandal is an octagonal three-storeyed monument with a narrow balcony running all around the second. On the third floor is an open pavilion with a parapet running around it. This is surmounted by a small eight-columned cupola, which is decorated with floral and geometric designs.

This monument is 60.5 feet high with a diameter of 52 feet and built of red sandstone with marble decoration. There are eight recessed pointed arches under the stone ledge of the upper storey on its eight sides.

Sher Mandal has one main room inside and four smaller ones on the side, which open into it. It was 'profusely ornamented with paintings of flowers and patterns in various colours, the patterns are very beautiful'. The colours used are blue, green, red, yellow, white, grey and black and the stairs are narrow and dangerous.[45]

I once climbed to the top of this building in the 1970s. I do remember being scared of the steps from which Emperor Humayun is said to have slipped and fallen to his death.

The place is famous for this historical legend. He is said to have made Sher Mandal his library and observatory; he was interested in astronomy.

Several medieval books describe his last evening.[46] Here is a gist:

Sher Mandal

Emperor Humayun came to this palace on the seventh Rabi Awwal. That night, Venus was to rise somewhat late and Emperor Humayun, as was his habit, went to the roof to observe the stars with his telescope. On his descent, he heard the muezzin call for maghrib prayers and sat down out of respect. He recited the prayers the faithful are meant to, on hearing the azan:

> *'Allahumma Rabba hadhihi-d-da' watit-tammati was-salatil qa'imati, ati Mohammadan al-Wasilata wal-Fadilata, wab' athhu Maqaman Mahmudan-il-ladhi wa' adtahu; Innaka la tukhleful meaadh.'*

This translates to:

> 'O Allah! Lord of this perfect call and of the regular prayer which is going to be established. Kindly give Mohammad

(saws) the right of intercession and superiority and bestow upon him (saws) the Maqaam am-Mahmuda (a station of Praise and Glory) which You promised him; verily, You never ever go against Your Promises.'

As he got up with the help of his staff, he slipped. He tumbled down headlong and died on the thirteenth Rabi Awwal, 19 January 1556, from his injuries.

Later day historians refute this theory, saying the staircase is winding and he could not have fallen from it. Mountstuart Elphinstone and John Clark Marshman say that he fell down headlong from the parapet of the roof.[47]

The chronogram for his death is:

'Humayun Badshah az baam uftad'
Emperor Humayun fell down from the roof.

This gives credence to the fact that he fell from the roof not stairs.

Shergarh/Dilli Sher Shahi

Zamaane ki gardish se chaara nahin hai
Zamaana hamara tumhara nahin hai
No one can escape time
Time waits for noone

Ibrat Mahroom

According to Abbas Khan in *Tarikh e Sher Shahi*, Emperor Sher Shah razed the older capital city that was near the river and built it on the banks of Yamuna. He gave orders for two forts to be built inside that city, though only one mosque and part of the walls were completed by the time of his death.

This city was to be built between Firozabad and Kilokri and named Shergarh. Two gates, one called Darwaza Sher Shahi (just opposite Purana Qila) and Lal Darwaza or Khooni Darwaza (near Firoz Shah Kotla), survive. This city was already in ruins in 1628 AD. According to a traveller De Laet, 'many houses were down and about twenty handsome Pathan monuments, in and out of the city, were more or less in decay'.

Kos Minar (Zoo) and Jasola

Koocha e yaar jo na jaata ho
Raasta raasta nahin hota
That which does not go to the Beloved's house
Cannot be called a road by any one

Ibn e Mufti

Elaborate arrangements were made by every ruler for messengers, who were the lifeblood of empires. Emperor Sher Shah regulated provisions for messengers with far reaching reforms.

Kos Minar was a medieval milestone installed on main roads to mark distance, a scheme adopted by the Mughals after Emperor Sher Shah. These were useful especially for travellers and 'dak' runners (postmen). Emperor Sher Shah also built the road today known as Grand Trunk Road, with trees on either side for shade.

The Arabic word 'bareed' (which also means 12 miles) is still used for a messenger and 'dak' means post. There were two types of dak services under the Mughals. Horseback service (costing 4 kos) was known as 'aulakh'. On foot, there were pavilions for 'harkaras' (or messengers) at every third of a mile,

Kos Minar - Zoo

like a relay service. A *harkara* would have a two-yard stick with copper bells on his head and run with envelopes. Each one-mile distance was called a 'karwa' and the station for the messengers were known as 'dawas'.

Criminals would also be transported on cots in this manner. This service even included transportation of dry fruits for the emperor as well as Ganga water. A Kos Minar, now inside the Delhi Zoo, was entered from the eastern side of Purana Qila. It was located near Azim Ganj ki Sarai (Sundar Nagar Nursery).

A Kos Minar has four parts with the bottom being octagonal and tapering in a circular form to the top, culminating in a small round head. These were placed all over to mark the distance, usually adjoining *sarais*. There is one standing in the middle of a small park in Jasola behind Apollo hospital.

Khair-ul-Manazil/Maham Begum ka Madrasa

Gar dil mein chashm e beena ho
Butkhana ho yaa Kaaba ho
Har ghar mein hain issi ke darshan
SubhanAllah SubhanAllah
If one has the vision
Whether in a temple or Kaaba
You will see the Divine everywhere
Subhan Allah Subhan Allah[48]

This mosque and madrasa is opposite the Purana Qila and was built by Emperor Akbar's wet nurse, Maham Anga, in 1561 AD. The madrasa probably fell into disuse by the twentieth century, but the mosque is still functional. The ruins of the madrasa are impressive. It was once quite ornamented, with coloured plaster and glazed tiles. Flowers painted in blue, white, yellow, purple, red and green ornamented darwazas.

The current imam of the mosque is Janab Basheer Ahmed, now in his late eighties. He has even seen the transfer of power from the British to independent India! In the late nineteenth and early twentieth centuries, a popular pastime in the mosque involved shooting at the roof of the mosque for echoes. This has not helped the mosque's state.

There used to be a huge neem tree outside the gateway with the grave of a pir of which no traces remain. Behind the mosque were ruins of many houses and mansions near the Dilli Sher Shahi Darwaza, which were probably ruins of the city. The old Johri Bazar or marketplace used to run till the late twentieth century.

In 1564 AD an attempt was made on Akbar's life from the roof of this madrasa. *Tabaqat e Akbari* says that Mirza Sharfuddin Hussain rebelled against Akbar and went towards Nagaur. Here he conspired with Shah Abul Ma'ali and

Khair-ul-Manazil/ Maham Begum ka Madrasa

with 300 loyalists he tried to hide. One of these loyalists was an Abysinnian slave named Koka Faulad Habshi, who had pledged to kill Emperor Akbar. He managed to infiltrate the royal camp and waited for a suitable moment to fulfil his vow.

One day, Emperor Akbar went to pay his respects to Hazrat Nizamuddin Auliya's dargah after a day of hunting. When he was returning from the dargah, he passed by this madrasa and felt something pierce his arm and saw that it was an arrow. By God's grace, the injury was not serious. His soldiers immediately captured Faulad Habshi and brought him to the Emperor and killed him. Akbar did not give him a chance to confess as he said that he might unnecessarily name people and point the finger of suspicion towards innocent people. Akbar continued unperturbed towards the Qila and soon recovered from his injury and left for Agra.

Dargah Bibi Fatima Sam

> *When a lion comes out of the jungle no one asks if it's a male or female. The children of Adam must obey and show respect, whether it is male or female.*
>
> *Hazrat Nizamuddin Auliya for Bibi Fatima Sam*

Not much is known about Bibi Fatima Sam except that she was the adopted sister of Baba Farid and her dargah in the midst of the residential area of Kakanagar is an oasis of peace. It is said that Bibi always answers the prayers of a mother and I often go there to pray, especially for my children.

The dargah, when made in the thirteenth century (probably around 1245 AD), was originally on the outskirts of Inderpat village, near the Nakhas Gate of Delhi. It was a sprawling complex that had a mosque attached to it as well as a small pond. It used to consist of merely a roof built over her grave. In 2002, Muhammed Adil, a businessman from Daryaganj, commissioned the new domed structure but it is restricted to just a small compound. A government school has been made between the dargah and the mosque.

Bibi Fatima Sam was a very pious lady and Baba Farid used to consider her his sister. Hazrat Nizamuddin Auliya often came to her dargah when he wanted complete peace.

Dargah Bibi Fatima Sam

Bibi Fatima was popularly known as Bibi Sam or Samina. She was said to be the Pir-Bahen or spiritual sister of Hazrat Nizamuddin Auliya and it won't be surprising if she used to be a disciple of Baba Farid, the Spiritual Master of Hazrat Nizamuddin Auliya.

Sheikh Gesu Daraz writes in his *malfuzat* that once Hazrat Roshan Chiragh e Dilli heard someone mention her name. He told a story which is most probably autobiographical. He said that after her death, Bibi Fatima Sam appeared in someone's dreams. He said, 'Once I was rushing into Allah's presence when an angel called out to her and said, "Wait! Where are you going so fearlessly?" She said that she stopped right there and sat down in the same spot. She vowed that she would not move till Allah Himself called her. In a few moments she saw Umm-ul Momineen (Mother of the Believers) Hazrat Khadija and her daughter, Hazrat Fatima, coming towards her. When they came close she embraced their feet. They asked, "O Fatima Sam, what is the matter that Allah Himself has sent us to call you?" She replied, "I am your slavegirl and there is no bigger honour for me than that you have come to call me. But I have vowed that I will not move from here till Allah Himself calls me." At that moment, a voice echoed in heaven, "O Fatima Sam, come to me. Tell me what do you want?" Fatima Sam replied, "O Allah there are such people in Your durbar who don't allow the ardent believers to come close to You."'

The *mutawalli* of the dargah patiently answered all my questions about the Bibi. I saw a few people praying there and I too wanted to pray. I was a bit apprehensive as there was only one room with the main shrine and most *mutawallis* of dargahs have reservations about women. He very politely told me to pray in the corner of the room hidden from view by the shrine so I would not be disturbed. I am glad that at least in a dargah of a lady, ladies are respected and treated at par. One of the advantages of these dargahs not being very popular is that there are no crowds and one can pray and meditate in peace. The *mutawalli* told me that at night jinns come and pray here. Also, you can visit only if Bibi wills you to do so as it is believed that no uninvited person can come here. The adjoining wall leads to the government school and across the street from the school is a small mosque known as Masjid Fatima Sam.

Bibi Fatima Sam reposed great faith in Hazrat Najibuddin Mutawakkil, the brother of Baba Farid and a great saint of the era; in fact, she was a devotee. He treated her as his sister. When there was nothing in the house to eat, she used to send some bread. Once she sent only one loaf. He said in jest: 'O, great God! Make the sultan of this city acquainted with our condition, so that he may send us something substantial!' Then he smiled and said: 'Alas! The sultans do not possess that inward cleanliness by which they may be acquainted (with our condition).'

Bibi Fatima is called the Rabia of Delhi, after Rabia of Basra, the famous mystic of the eighth century. Her *urs* is on eighteenth Shabaan. This dargah is located in Kaka Nagar.

Bhairon Mandir

> *The lotus is greeting the rising sun and the lily has closed its petals;*
> *Wearing their saffron robes and ashes, the ascetics are on their way to the holy temple to sound the auspicious conch*
>
> *Andal*[49]

There are two famous temples situated next to the northern walls of the Purana Qila, both said to be from the time of the Pandavas, though the buildings are modern. One is Dudhiya Bhairav Mandir where only milk is offered to the angry incarnation of Shiva, known as Rudra. The main temple is on the right, known as Pandav Kaleen Sri Kilkari Bhairav Mandir.

Legend says it was constructed by the Pandavs when they constructed the capital of Indraprastha. One legend about this deity is that Bhairav tried to enter a cave in which Vaishno Devi was inside. The goddess beheaded him but when he pleaded for mercy, she forgave him and left him as an idol that generations would worship. The idol in the temple is only up to the neck.

Bhairon Mandir

Another legend says that the temple is on the site Bhairav guarded when Bhim, a Pandav brother, performed a yagna for deliverance from the demons. The demon Bhairav was said to be fond of alcohol, the offering or prasad made here. The temple has a well called 'Pandabon ka Kuan'. The water from this well is believed to have curative powers and devotees ask for this water from the temple staff.

The temple is popular with tantriks. Though its present structure is only sixty years old, the site has been considered holy for over 3,500 years. Since Lord Bhairav's *vaahan* (vehicle) was a dog, all dogs in the area are left unharmed.

Emperor Humayun's Tomb

VII

Humayun's Tomb and Surrounding Area

Emperor Humayun's Tomb

Barapullah

Sadiyo'n sadiyo'n mera safar
Manzil manzil rahguzar
My journey goes on forever
Every destination a path

Jan Nisar Akhtar

Today, the Barapullah is a massive modern flyover. The original bridge was built by Meherban Agha Khwaja Sara over a stream of the Yamuna in 1612 AD. The original bridge had 11 arches and the name came from its 12 pillars. The Khwaja Sara was a trusted aide of Emperor Jahangir. He looked after the

Barapullah

palace and, had earned the emperor's respect. When Emperor Jahangir moved to Delhi in his sunset years, he instructed the governor of Delhi to ensure he had all the comforts of life in the city, which is when this bridge was built.

A few inscriptions in verse name the Khwaja Sara as the builder and give us the date of construction, along with praise for the emperor. There is an inscription with a few verses on it that give the date of construction. It was made of lime mortar and stone, and is now an unkempt market near the Hazrat Nizamuddin railway station. The bridge itself is in poor condition, with all twelve pillars encroached on by houses built on its edges. Only my determination helped me find all of them.

Tomb of Abdur Rahim Khan e Khana'n

Rahiman dhaaga prem kaa, mat todo chatakaay.
Tute se phir naa milai, milai gaanth padi jaay
Rahim says, don't snap the thread of love suddenly
Even if joined with difficulty, the knot remains

Rahim

Abdur Rahim Khan e Khana'n, famed for his *dohas*, was of Turkish descent. His grandfather, Saifuddin Ali Kosha Ismail, had been in the service of Emperor Babur and his father Bairam Khan e Khana'n held a high rank in the reign of Emperor Humayun. Bairam Khan e Khana'n was a guardian to Emperor Akbar and instrumental in his victory in the second Battle of Panipat in 1556 AD. When he died on his way to the Hajj in 1561 AD, his son, Abdur Rahim, was brought back to the court, raised under Emperor Akbar's guidance and nicknamed Mirza Khan.

Abdur Rahim also earned the title of Khan e Khana'n, being part of Emperor Akbar's *nauratan* (nine gems, important members of his court). He tutored Prince Salim, who later ascended the throne as Jehangir. Abdur Rahim Khan e Khana'n is credited with the translation of *Waqeat e Baburi*

Tomb of Abdur Rahim Khan e Khana'n

from Chaghtai to Persian. This tomb, originally built for his wife, was where he ended up in 1627 AD. What was originally a marble tomb was probably repurposed for other buildings.

Sir Syed wrote that it was removed during the rule of Nawab Asfud-Daula in Awadh and taken and sold in Lucknow. This was presumably because construction was going on in full swing in Lucknow and marble was not easy to procure because of its distance to Rajasthan. According to Basheeruddin Ahmad, the tomb was raided for red sandstone and marble slabs when canals were built on the river Yamuna.

Maal e muft
Dil e beraham
Free loaders are stone hearted

The tomb looks like a plucked hen. The Aga Khan Trust for Culture has taken up the task of restoring the monument's beautiful marble 'pichi kaari' (or mosaic) work.

There were many inscriptions on the mihrabs in the Tughra script but, inscribed as they were in lime, they have been destroyed. It is said to have had Quranic ayat and the Kalima, along with names of Allah.

The chronogram 'Khan Sipahsalar' gives the date of his death. Villagers lived in the tomb in the late nineteenth and twentieth centuries. When the British government made a list of protected monuments under the ASI, the tomb was in such a bad state that they did not include it in the list.

Sir Syed wrote, very poignantly, that one must never be foolish enough to place importance on worldly things, as one whose houses were showered with rose petals now lies under mud with the stink of urine and cow dung. Even the tombstone was stolen.

Fa'tabirû yâ oulî al absâr
Take warning, then, O ye, with intelligence

Quran 59 :2

Sabz Burj

Bujhti huyi shammo'n par
Mehrab huye haath
Flickering lamps
Protected by cusped hand

Nazeer Qaiser

This structure stands at the intersection of Mathura Road and Lodi Road, near the complex of Emperor Humayun's Tomb.

Zafar Hasan says that the drum of the dome was originally decorated in green, yellow and blue tiles, from which it got its name Sabz Burj. When the structure was repaired, the dome was made blue but one can still see green and yellow on recessed bays.

Sabz Burj

In 1902, H.C. Fanshawe called it 'Sabz Posh' which he took to mean Green Top because of the colour of its dome.[50] This structure is also sometimes called Nili Chatri, which is a misnomer. The actual Nili Chatri was Naubat Khan's tomb and was demolished at some point of time.

The Sabz Burj is built on the lines of 'musamman Baghdadi' or a chamfered octagon. What remains tells us the original tile work must have been exquisite. Basheeruddin Ahmad said that it might have been a tomb from the Saiyyid dynasty, as it was known as 'Saiyyado'n ka maqbara'.

The grave within still existed till 1919 but was removed when it was made into a police station at a later day by the British. Today it is a landmark, marking a busy square with roads leading to Lodi Road, Emperor Humayun's tomb and the dargah of Hazrat Nizamuddin Auliya.

Sunder Nursery

Daag e gham dil par utha kar marne waale mar gaye
Burj qabro'n ke agar sarv e chiragha'n ho'n to kya
They took the wounds of life on their hearts and left this world
So what if the light of the lamps on the grave flicker till the sky

Muneer Shikohabadi

This nursery used to be a *sarai* built by Azim Khan, extending to Dinpanah or Purana Qila and the ruins of Azim Khan's haveli inside the zoo. Called Azimganj (which means bazaar), it might have housed the workers constructing Emperor Humayun's tomb. Delhi had extensive construction at the time. It was on the road between Agra and Delhi and was a centre of activity during Mughal times before the court and capital shifted to Shahjahanabad. It might also have served as a place for travellers to stay.

This extensive and well-built walled enclosure was known by government servants as 'Sarai Mughliya'. Its walls, including the battlements, were 28.5 feet high. It was a famous *sarai* from the Mughal times, with four lofty darwazas, none of which remain today. It occupied a space of 430 square feet. The villagers who evacuated Purana Qila in 1919 came and settled here. *Sarais* fell into disuse after the railways. A portion of this area was taken over for agriculture. This *sarai* is now taken care of by the government and is known as Sunder Nursery.

Mughal Mihrab

Thay ghaib ke teshe se taraashe huye hum tab
Angdaai ki surat teri mehrab mein aaye
Since the chisel of the unseen fashioned us out, then
We descended into your vault, with a languorous twirl

Riyaz Latif

It was a custom to build mosques within *sarais* and the ruins of the one at Azimganj are seen in the Sunder Nursery. Though decrepit now, the lofty mihrab speaks of the original purpose. The mosque is on a plinth with steps leading up to it and is one of the prettiest places I have seen.

The courtyard is 6 feet above the ground and used to be enclosed by walls of 9 feet 4 inches in height and furnished with arched openings. One can see the stumps of arches in the photograph.

Mughal Mehrab

The romantic in me can visualise the niche for incense, smell the sweet fragrance, imagine the flicker of lamps in the wind for worshippers. The atmosphere must have been ethereal. I wish I could light a lamp here but, not wanting to disturb the environment, I left the place with a prayer for the departed souls resting in such a tranquil place.

Sundarwala Mahal and Bagh

Ai junoon tere vaaste sab hain
Baagh kis ka hai, raagh kis ka hai
O frenzy everything is for you
Whose is the garden? Whose is the villa?

Wazir Ali Saba Lakhnavi

There are three monuments inside Sundar Mahal: the Sundarwala Mahal, the Sundarwala Burj and Lakkarwala Burj. These monuments were treated quite badly when villagers lived in them; cooking and cow dung has left lasting damage.

The Sundarwala Burj was said to have been decorated with beautiful floral designs and calligraphy. Its finial has fallen down and one can see an abrupt lotus without the culminating finial. Locals of the twentieth century used the doorframes and wood of the place for their own houses.

Basheeruddin Ahmad describes the inscription on this place as being the best in Delhi.

The Lakkarwala Gumbad is 38 square feet from outside. It had six graves in it. The interior of the tomb had calligraphic inscription. There is no date or name inscribed to give any clue to its builder or the persons buried inside.

The Aga Khan Trust for Culture has recently restored these monuments.

Sundarwala Mahal and Bagh

Hazrat Patte Shah ki Dargah

Hazrat Patte Shah ki Dargah

> *Khabaram raseed imshab ki nigaar khuahi aamad;*
> *Sar-e man fidaa-e raah-e ki sawaar khuahi aamad*
> *There came the news that tonight, you, my beloved, would come*
> *May my head be sacrificed to the road along which you will come*
> *Hazrat Amir Khusrau*

There are two graves on the platform. An inscription on the left grave gives us the name Hazrat Shamsuddin. The other one does not have any inscription and, according to Basheeruddin Ahmad, is famous as Mamu Bhanja ki dargah. His nephew is buried along with him in a double grave.

The entrance to the dargah is a grand gateway of Mughal vintage. A modern masjid is built inside it as well as the grave of Abdul Qadir, which was built in 1958. The entrance to the saint's shrine is through a low door in the left corner of the courtyard. The construction of the grave is modern but the low entrance and walls seem of an older time.

There are different accounts regarding Hazrat Shamsuddin Utawala. He is said to have been either a saint of the Suhrawardi silsila or a *mureed* (disciple) of Hazrat Turkman Bayabani. In one place, it is mentioned he was the *mureed* of Hazrat Qutubuddin Bakhtiyar Kaki.

The name Shamsuddin Utawala suggest the word 'impatient' was a title he earned; Hazrat Nizamuddin Auliya and others are said to have sent people to him for quick fulfilment of wishes. He was a great saint of his time, with many miracles to his credit. It was his habit to light a fire and sit on its ashes. He would lie at night inside the ash of a grave he built for himself. It is said that the saint avoided Hazrat Nizamuddin Auliya, saying that his *duniyaavi jah o jalaal* (worldly grandeur) was too much for his own reclusive nature. But he wished for his burial and funeral to be conducted by Hazrat Nizamuddin Auliya, which happened in 1300 AD.

There is an ancient Pilu tree in the compound and it is said that anybody who eats a leaf from the branches will have her wishes fulfilled. This is why the saint was given the name 'Patte Shah'.[51] When I visited, the present-day khadim gave me a sugar candy wrapped in a leaf and a rose. An old lady who came to pray here told me that the old tree growing there looked like the Urdu alphabets that spelt the word Mohammad in Arabic.

Bare Batashewala or Batashe ka Mahal

Pattharo'n par naqsh ubhra kyun nahin
Dast e be-tesha ne socha kyun nahin
Wonder why the marks didn't show up on the stones
Why didn't the hands without the chisel think of this?

Tasawwur Zaidi

This is opposite the dargah of Hazrat Patte Shah and was recently restored by the Aga Khan Trust for Culture. Though it is famous as Batashe ka Mahal, it is the tomb of Mirza Muzaffar, Emperor Akbar's son-in-law. This tomb is

Bare Batashewala

beautifully decorated by floral designs incised in plaster. The pattern on the ceiling is exquisite. The central room has 20 feet 10 inches by 7 feet concrete strips, attractively decorated with floral designs and having an inscription with details on Mirza Muzaffar. No one knows why this place was called Batashewala. It is possible that it was named after a garden in which it was located.

Chhote Batashewala

Jaane tab kyun suraj ki khvaahish karte hain log
Jab baarish mein sab diwaare'n girne lagti hain
I wonder why people crave for the sun only when
All the walls start falling in the rains

Salim Kauser

This is the ruins of a tomb and has been recently restored by Aga Khan Trust for Culture.

Emperor Humayun's Tomb

> *'As for the righteous, they will be in the midst of gardens and rivers, in and assembly of truth, in the presence of a Sovereign Omnipotent.'*
>
> *[Surat al-Qamar, 54: 54-55]*

Paradise as described in the Quran will have rivers of milk and honey and gardens with trees in it. In fact, the word 'jannat' (or paradise) means a garden set with trees, surrounded by eight principal gates.

There are eight levels of Paradise and man is not allowed on the seventh and last level called 'al-arsh' (allegorical for God's throne). This led to the concept of 'hasht bihisht' (or Eight Heavens) for funerary monuments. Hasht-bihisht is a Persian architectural term which refers to a specific type of floor plan, divided into eight chambers that surround a central room. These tombs were square or rectangular planned buildings, divided into nine sections such that a central domed chamber is surrounded by eight elements.

The flowing rivers in Persian and Mughal tombs are modelled on the four rivers which flow in *jannat*, namely Saihan (Syr dariya), Jaihan (Amu dariya), Furat (Euphrates) and Nil (Nile), and a spring named Salsabeel which is the source of the Rivers of Rahma (mercy) and Kausar (abundance). All this imagery is supposed to help the soul of the dead man gain forgiveness and entry into Paradise.

Emperor Humayun's tomb was the first tomb built on this Persian principle of 'Char Bagh' or paradisiacal tombs. The tomb, when built, was surrounded by gardens with cypress trees and flowerbeds. There were water canals flowing all around it, with fountains flowing in the *hauz* at intervals. The *hauz* and water channels are still there and all but the central one do not work. The garden had become completely desolate in the nineteenth and twentieth centuries and, for a brief time, was used for agricultural cultivation. Lord Curzon, responsible for saving many of India's architectural treasures, helped preserve Emperor Humayun's tomb.

Emperor Humayun's Tomb

Har ke mi khwahad ke binad shakl e Firdaus e Bareen
Go baya een Qasr wa een Bagh e Humayun ra ba-been
Anybody who wants to have a glimpse of Heaven on Earth,
Should be invited to see this tomb and garden of Humayun Badshah[52]

Emperor Humayun died on 21 January 1555 and was buried in Kilokri. His wife, Haji Begum, built this tomb and interred him here.

There is a lot of confusion about the identity of Haji Begum, the builder of this tomb. Was she Bega Begum, Emperor Humayun's first wife, or Hamida Bano Begum, the last? Sir Syed identifies Haji Begum as Hamida Bano Begum, the mother of Emperor Akbar. Gulbadan Begum, the writer of *Humayun Nama*, identifies Haji Begum as Bega Begum, Emperor Humayun's first cousin and first wife. A reference from 1696 AD identifies her as Emperor

Akbar's stepmother, so it is clear that Haji Begum and Hamida Bano Begum are two different persons.

In the *Indian Travels of Therenot and Carri,* we find this: 'Upon the road from Agra to Bayana there is a royal house built by the queen mother (step) of Eebar [Emperor Akbar] with gardens kept in very good order.'[53]

The *Humayun Nama* also mentions: 'She remained there with the other ladies when Emperor Humayun made this expedition to recover Hindustan, and she came with Hamida and Gul-Badan and the rest to join Emperor Akbar in 964 AH (1557 AD). After this she built her husband's tomb near Dihli, and became its faithful attendant.'

I think the confusion may have arisen from the fact that, although Emperor Akbar was extremely fond of her, Haji Begum was not Emperor Humayun's favourite. He left her behind after his defeat in the Battle of Chausa, where she was taken captive by Emperor Sher Shah, who had her escorted with full honour to Emperor Humayun's camp in Agra later.

The construction of Emperor Humayun's tomb was started in 1562–63 AD. It took eight to nine years to complete it and cost 15 lakh rupees at the time. Most of the expense was borne by Emperor Akbar.

The chief architect of these tombs was Mir Mirak Ghiyas of Herat, identified as a stonecutter in Emperor Babur's memoirs. He had worked extensively in Bukhara and his area of speciality was buildings and landscape architecture. He died before the tomb was completed and his son Saiyyed Mohammed completed the project in 1571 AD.

This tomb is also the dormitory of the Timurids, with over 150 royals of that family buried here. This is the only tomb in the world to have the graves of so many emperors, queens, princes and princesses. It is one of the most magnificent monuments of India and perhaps the world. Despite its size, it is delicate and beautifully symmetrical.

This was the first grand tomb of the Mughals and influenced all the others that followed. It is the first distinct example of proper Mughal style, which was inspired by Persian architecture. The tomb proper stands in the centre of a square garden, divided into four main parterres by causeways, in the centre of which ran shallow water channels. The high rubble-built enclosure is entered via two lofty double-storeyed gateways on the west and south. A *baradari* (pavilion) occupies the centre of the eastern wall and a hammam in the centre of northern wall.

The square red sandstone double-storeyed structure of the mausoleum with chamfered corners rises from a seven-metre high square terrace, raised over a series of cells, which are accessible through arches on each side. The grave proper in the centre of this cell-complex is reached by a passage on the south. The octagonal central chamber contains the cenotaph and the diagonal sides lead to corner-chambers, which house the graves of other members of the royal family. Externally, each side of the tomb and its elevations are decorated by marble borders and panels and dominated by three arched alcoves, the central one being the highest. Over the roof, pillared kiosks are disposed around the high emphatic double dome in the centre. The central octagonal chamber contains the cenotaph, surrounded by octagonal chambers on the sides. Perforated screens are placed on the windows. There are three arches on each side with the central one being larger. This plan is repeated on the second storey. The roof surmounted by a double dome (42.5 metre) of marble has pillared *chhatris* (kiosks) placed around it.

This mausoleum is a perfect blend of Persian architecture and Indian traditions. While Sikandar Lodi's tomb was the first garden-tomb to be built in India, it was Emperor Humayun's tomb that went on to become a template, resulting in the Taj Mahal at Agra. There is also a somewhat common human angle to both monuments: one erected by a devoted wife for her husband and the other by an equally devoted husband for his wife.

The tomb has two magnificent gateways, a western and a southern one. The western darwaza which we use today is unparalleled in its attractiveness and elegance. It has apartments on top, which must have once housed the people who took care of it. Every apartment has a different entrance and stairs.

The southern darwaza has arches and platforms. Sir Syed likens the two gates to the Gates of Heaven. They were built of red sandstone and 'sang e rukham' (alabaster) used to look like marble. The waterworks for the streams and fountains were housed in a pavilion in the eastern wall which bordered the river Yamuna. They can be seen from the Damdama Gurudwara. The British used the southern gateway as a 'Dar-ul-Iqama' or rest house. The officers who came here to visit it would stay in it.

This complex houses the graves of Hamida Bano Mariyam Makani, Mohammad Azam Shah, Emperors Farukhsiyar, Jahandar Shah, Rafi-ud-Daula and Alamgir II. But perhaps the most important is the tomb of Dara Shukoh.

Dara Shukoh was killed very close to this tomb in a Kilokri palace, where he had been imprisoned and beheaded, and was later buried here. This is also famous as Emperor Bahadur Shah Zafar's last place of refuge in 1857.

Barber's Tomb

Woh gulshano'n ke baaghba'n, woh wajah e raunaq e jahan
Uthi'n jo unki mayyate'n, koi nahin tha nauha khwa'n
Those who tended the rose gardens, who were the light of the world
When their funeral was held, there were no mourners, young or old
Ajmal Siddiqui

This is a domed tomb in the south-eastern corner of Emperor Humayun's tomb. Though it is alternatively referred to as 'Saqqa' (water carrier) or 'Hajjam [or barber] ka maqbara', no one knows who is buried here. There is speculation that it could be Emperor Humayun's brother, Kamran. It has two graves, and the *takhti* and *qalam* denote that they are that of a male and female. Though Quranic ayat are inscribed on them, no name is written on it. Sir Syed has fixed its date of construction at 1780 AD but gives no reference to his sources.

Barber's Tomb

Afsarwala Tomb and Masjid

Tum se pahle wo jo ek shakhs yahan takht-nashin tha
Usko bhi apne Khuda hone pe itna hi yaqeen tha
The man who sat on this throne before you
He was convinced that he is God, too

Habib Jalib

These are inside the Emperor Humayun's tomb complex and built as a pair. The octagonal tomb houses four unknown graves. The mosque is a three-arched single aisle, popular in the Lodi and Mughal eras. The two are built close to one another on a common platform. There are calligraphic inscriptions and remnants of inscribed plaster medallions. The staircases on either side of the mosque are in terrible condition. There are remains of rooms that must have contained a flourishing madrasa.

Afsarwala Tomb and Masjid

Arab Sarai

Nikalna khuld se aadam ka sunte aaye hain lekin
Bahut be-aabru hokar tere kuuche se ham nikle
Am familiar with stories of Adam's expulsion from Paradise yet,
Very dishonourable was my exit from your street

Mirza Ghalib

This was a walled enclosure built in 1560 AD by Haji Begum. Only one of the three gateways to it survive. It has been restored by the Aga Khan Trust for Culture.

It is said that the Begum brought 300 Arabs from Harmain Shahrif (in Mecca): 100 from elite Saiyyid families, 100 Sheikhs or people well-versed in religion and 100 ordinary men for day-to-day service. Descendants from this line still live in Delhi. I once met a gentleman in Hazrat Nizamuddin Basti claiming to be a descendant of such Arabs. There used to be three Gateways to this Sarai but now only one remains. It's very lofty and has been restored by Aga Khan Trust for Culture.

Arab Sarai Mandi

Hai ab is maamure mein qaht-e gham-e ulfat Asad
Hum ne ye maana ke Dilli mein rahe'n khave'nge kya
A famine of the grief of love, engulfs this town, Asad
We have agreed that if we remain in Delhi- what will we eat?

Mirza Ghalib

On entering from the northern gateway of Arab Sarai, we can see the ruins of another walled compound with a darwaza. Basheeruddin Ahmad said that this had an elegant mosque, of which nothing remains. The *baoli* attached to it remains.

It is a beautiful *baoli*, attracting many curious visitors. It is still filled with water and one has to be careful when looking into it. An eastern gateway is kept locked, which has remnants of tile work and an inscription indicating the name of the builder and period. Meherban Agha Khwaja Sara built this *mandi* during the reign of Emperor Jahangir during along with the Barapullah Bridge.

Garden of Bu Halima

Gulo'n mein rang bhare baad e naubahaar chale
Chale bhi aao ke gulshan ka karobaar chale
Let the breeze of a new spring, flow and fill the flowers with colours
Please do come so that the garden can get on with its daily business

Faiz Ahmed Faiz

Today one enters Emperor Humayun's tomb from a gap in the western wall of this garden.

The garden is enclosed on three sides with a lovely *burj* on the corner. One can still see the tile work on it. A flat-roofed structure stands in this garden, said to be the tomb of Bu Halima. Not much is known about her.

Tomb and Masjid of Isa Khan Niazi

Ibn e Mariyam huwa kare koi
Mere dukh ki dawa kare koi
Let someone be the son of Mary
A [messiah] is one who can cure me of my pain

Mirza Ghalib

Isa Khan was a notable and trusted noble in Emperor Sher Shah's court. He had aided Salim Shah in the war of succession after Emperor Sher Shah and it

Tomb of Isa Khan

was because of his support and able guidance that Salim Shah could defeat his elder brother, Adil Khan.

This walled enclosure housing the mosque and tomb is called Isa Khan ka Kotla. It has 128 recessed niches in the enclosing wall. These were built in 1547 AD during the reign of Sultan Salim Shah. The location is a favourite spot for tourists who like to wander to the top to get a better view of the area.

The mosque, measuring 88 feet × 30.5 inches, is built of quartzite and lime mortar with red sandstone on the facade and mihrabs. It stands on a plinth that makes it higher than the tomb, which must have been intentional. Close to the third archway on the southwest corner of the mosque is a well that may at some point have fed a tank for ablutions. So many changes have been made in medieval monuments, especially the flooring, that we don't really know the original designs.

The facade and dome had tile work and, despite the passage of time and the vagaries of nature, some of the blue tiles still survive. It turns out our ancestors knew how to make permanent structures! The monument is undergoing repairs under the aegis of the Aga Khan Trust for Culture.

Isa Khan built the tomb in his own lifetime and it is one of the finest examples of octagonal tombs. Though these were normally reserved for royalty under the Lodis and Pathans, maybe Khan's position entitled him to one too.

Villagers occupied this tomb during the latter part of nineteenth and the early twentieth century.

Chilla of Hazrat Nizamuddin Auliya

> *The day that you appeared like the moon, did you not know that you would be the place to which the world looks up?*[54]

This chillahgah of Hazrat Nizamuddin Auliya is behind Humayun's tomb. A *chillahgah* is the place where saints reside and observe their spiritual devotions. Not much of it remains today but whatever there is gives a sense of peace and belonging.

A 9 feet x 8 feet room still remains at the back with a lamp burning in a niche. There is a small mosque and a courtyard, which contains some graves.

Hazrat Nizamuddin Auliya lived in many houses in Delhi on rent, including the house of Hazrat Amir Khusrau's maternal grandfather, Rawat Arz in Mehrauli. One day he met a Darwesh who advised him to leave the hustle and bustle of the city and go to a secluded place where he could devote his time to prayers. Hazrat Nizamuddin was determined to leave the city but it took twenty-five years to eventually shift from there. One day he went to Jasrat ka Bagh in Hauz Rani and after his prayers, prayed to God for guidance, as he wanted to go wherever God willed. There he received the divine revelation that his place was in Ghiyaspur. He had not heard of this place before and so he went to his friend's house to find that his friend, Naqeeb Nishapuri had been to Ghiyaspur. Later he went to Ghiyaspur with his friend to find it uninhabited and away from the city and started living there.

When Sultan Kaikobad built the city of Kilokri, many nobles shifted here and Ghiyaspur too saw an influx of residents. The saint wanted to shift from here as his prayers were getting interrupted. A handsome young man came to him and said that actual remembrance of Allah, devotion to him, was that which was done in the midst of people, and despite disturbance, not in

Chillah of Hazrat Nizamuddin

total solitude. The saint immediately gave up his intention and spent the rest of his life there in the house on the bank of River Jamuna. This mysterious man is said to be Khizr, the Prophet, who is immortal and is said to be a spiritual guide of Moses and Prophet Mohammad. Years later, Hazrat Nizamuddin told his friends that he cherished that moment as one of the most precious in his life.

It was a tiled house and his mureed and dependants also lived there with him. The saint passed away in this house and was given his ghusl e janaza in it.

Nila Gumbad

Bas ek khandhar mere andar jiye hi jaata hai
Ajeeb haal hai maazi mein haal thahra hai
A ruin seems to keep on living within me
Strange is my condition that I am stuck in the past

Bilqis Zafirul Hasan

It is so called because of the blue glazed tile work on its dome. One of the finest examples of tile work called kaar-kashaani it had been very cruelly treated by time and some callous officials. The railway line passing next to it further added to its decay. The grave has also disappeared; maybe someone broke it in trying to steal the headstone.

Different colour tiles had been used all over this *burj* to make it a thing of beauty and Aga Khan Trust has lovingly restored it to a semblance of its former beauty. There are efforts afoot to take it into Emperor Humayun's tomb complex.

After Mahabat Khan had put Abdur Rahim Khan e Khana under house arrest via fraudulent means, he sent a message to Fahim Khan, who was his loyal courtier of Abdur Rahim Khan e Khana. Fahim refused to betray his master and died fighting along with his son and forty followers.

After being released from captivity, Abdur Rahim Khan e Khana got Fahim Khan's body from Agra and buried him here as Fahim Khan had considered this place sanctified probably due to the presence of Hazrat Nizamuddin's Dargah. He built this tomb in 1624 AD.

Nila Gumbad

Khan e Khana called him Miyan and that's how he was famous. Fahim Khan was the son of a Rajput and was brought up by Khan e Khana as his own son along with his own children. He was in charge of all of Khan e Khana's affairs and had complete controlover his revenues, which he discharged faithfully.

A famous saying resulted from this:

Kamaaye Khan e Khana'n
Aur lutaaye Miyan Fahim
Khan e Khana'n earns
And Miyan Fahim spends

The tomb is a chamfered octagon. As with other monuments, it was also used as a cattle shed by villagers sometime in the late nineteenth century. This monument is seen in a painting by Edwin Lord Weeks, captioned mistakenly as an 'Old Mosque in Delhi'. In this we see beautiful and intricate tile work ('chini ka kaam'), most of which has now been destroyed.

VIII

Hazrat Nizamuddin Basti

JUMPING WELL AT NIZAMODEEN R.A.
DEAHI

Baoli Hazrat Nizamuddin Auliya Dargah (Courtesy: ASI archives)

Barah Khamba

Marzi e yaar ke khilaaf na ho
Log mere liye dua na kare'n
Perchance it goes against my Beloved's will
Don't pray for my well-being

Hasrat Mohani

This is an old monument opposite Sabz Burj. It is a square building surmounted by a central dome, with four smaller domes on the sides. There are three arches with a width of 7 feet 2 inches, flanked by two smaller ones of a width of 5 feet 5 inches.

Dargah of Malik Yaar Parra'n

Tomb in Golf Course

Chillahgah of Hazrat Nizamuddin Auliya

Khirki Masjid

Yaadgar e Ustad Sheikh Ibrahim Zauq

Tomb of Isa Khan

Cenotaph of Safdar Jung (inside view)

Urs of Hazrat Nizamuddin Auliya

Bijai Mandal

Dargah of Matka Peer

Gateway of Adilabad fort

Tomb of Saiyyed Abid at Golf Course

Tomb outside National Stadium

Wall in Atgah Khan's tomb

Nila Gumbad

Dome of an encroached tomb in Zamaradpur

There is a gallery of 9 feet 3 inches wide running around the central hall, which is 30 feet 5 inches square. The four smaller domes are on the gallery while the central hall houses the main dome. This hall has three arches, each supported by the twelve columns from which it gets its name, Barah Khamba. The columns are of quartzite and the rest of the monument is of lime and mortar. The tile work on the dome has long since disappeared.

The tomb of the two graves within must be from the Lodi era. It was used as a madrasa under the Mughals and the British. It is said that Faizullah Khan Bangash had built his grave near this, which collapsed due to bad construction. It is now in a lovely park and is home to the many homeless of the area, who jump over the grills surrounding it. It has been restored recently by the Aga Khan Trust for Culture.

Lal Mahal

Keejiye aur koi zulm agar zid hai yahin
Leejiye aur meri lab pe duaaye'n aayin
If that's your wish, oppress me as much as you want
Lo! My lips move in some more prayers

Jigar Moradabadi

The Lal Mahal peeps over the boundary walls put in place by the Jamiat e Ulema e Hind, whose madrasa and mosque surrounds it. There are many theories about the purpose of Lal Mahal and the period during which it was built. Sir Syed wrote:

> Lal Mahal, which is referred to as Kushk e Lal by historians, is a building from the Khilji period. In the days when Alauddin Khilji had laid siege to the fort of Ranthambhor, Haji Maula Ghulamzada (son of a slave) Mulk-ul-Umara Fakhruddin Kotwal, rebelled and sat on the throne of Delhi, in this Kushk

Lal Mahal (Courtesy: ASI archives)

e Lal. Now there are no remnants of it and people have made these ruins famous as Lal Mahal. The surprising part is that this building contains graves. It's possible that there was a mahal near it and when that building was wiped out, the name Lal Mahal was transferred to this one. This building too is very ancient and has graves inside it. I can't say whose graves these are or who built it.

This might have been a place built for the rest of the royals who visited Hazrat Nizamuddin Auliya. A double-storeyed building with a central dome and four smaller cupolas on the sides was seen till the late twentieth century, as seen in photographs from the ASI archives. The upper floor was an open hall with arched openings. Its similarity to the Alai Darwaza led nineteenth century historians come to the conclusion that it was from the Khilji period. It was one of the first buildings in which *tykhana* or underground rooms were built. Only the dome now survives. Ibn Battuta stayed here in the fourteenth century.

The 800-year-old Lal Mahal is not a notified building, so access to it is not available to conservationists or even the ASI. In 2009, a four-member heritage conservation committee appointed by the Supreme Court was to inspect it but could not access it because the area was sealed off. Nothing came off a petition called #SaveLalMahal. I tried to visit the area with Syed Mohammad Qasim but members of the Jamiat e Ulema got very agitated when we tried to take photos.

Chausath Khamba

Ishq aamad az junoon bahreh mandam kard
Wa arasta ze sohbat khirad mandam kard
Azaad ze band e deen wa daanish gastham
Taa silsila e zulf kas e bandam kard
Love came and through passion was profitable to me
When love comes to you keep it away from intellect
I am freed from the captivity of religion and intelligence
And now someone's curls chain me

Mirza Aziz Kokaltash[55]

Mirza Aziz Kokaltash Khan, son of Khan e Azam Atgah Khan, died in Ahmedabad in 1624 AD during the the reign of Emperor Jahangir. His body was brought and buried near his father's tomb in the tomb known as Chausath Khamba, meaning '64 pillars'. The 64 pillars divide the area into 25 bays with domes on each bay. However, these are externally flat-roofed. Built completely of white marble, it is an exquisite building.

Chausath Khamba

Mirza Aziz Kokaltash obviously favoured beautiful buildings. For example, his house in the Agra fort was painted by the head of Emperor Akbar's painting atelier, Abd al Samad, and his tomb remains the finest Jahangir-period building in Delhi today.[56]

There are many questions about the peculiar shape of Chausath Khamba, especially since it was a mausoleum. It is possible that it was built as an eclectic hall for gatherings of family members who came to visit Hazrat Nizamuddin Auliya's dargah and Atgah Khan's tomb. Mirza Aziz Kokaltash Khan's marble grave is on a double platform and is exquisitely decorated with calligraphy. There are circular medallions on the grave with Quranic ayat inscribed on it. A tomb with a flat *takhti* (slate) suggests that the widow of Mirza Aziz Kokaltash Khan was buried here. Intricately carved jalis (marble screens) cover the walls of the hall. There are other graves, possibly of family members, buried here. The Aga Khan Trust for Culture has recently restored it.

Mirza Ghalib's Tomb

The famous poet Dabir-ul-Mulk, Najm-ud-Daula Mirza Asadullah Khan Ghalib died on 15 February 1869 AD. He was buried near the Dargah of Hazrat Nizamuddin Auliya in the graveyard belonging to the Nawabs of Loharu, to whom he was related via his mother and wife's family. It was a simple grave and only recognizable as the grave of a great poet because of the inscription on it:

Ya Hayyo Yaa Qayyum
Rashk e Urfi wa fakhr e talib murd
Asadullah Khan Ghalib Murd
Kal main gham o andoh mein ba khatir e mahzoon
Tha turbat e Ustad pe baitha huwa ghamnaak
Dekha to mujhe fikr mein tareekh ke, Majruh
Hatif ne kaha ganj e ma'ni hai tah e khaak
O Living, O Sustaining
The envy of Urfi and the pride of Talib is dead
Asadullah Khan Ghalib is dead
Yesterday I was distraught and grieving
I sat by the grave of my master,
As Majruh was pondering over a chronogram,
The guardian angel cried 'beneath the dust is a treasure of meaning'
Mir Mahdi Majruh, 1285 AH

According to Maulana Altaf Hussain Hali, he was buried at the foot of the grave of his father-in-law, Mirza Ilahi Bakhsh.

A marble tomb built by Aga Khan Trust for Culture replaced the old simple grave in 2010 AD.

Mirza Ghalib's Tomb

And seeing the drooping flowers put on his grave I recalled his verse

Huye mar ke hum jo ruswa, huye kyun na garq e darya
Na kabhi janaaza uthta, Na kahin mazaar hota
This ignomy after death, why wasn't I drowned in the river
Nor would my coffin been lifted, nowhere my tomb would be
Mirza Ghalib

Ghalib was born on 27 December 1797 AD and he saw the ups ad downs of life including the First War of Indian Independence and the end of the Mughal Empire.

His life was spent in impoverished circumstances, fighting for his pension and perpetually in debt but nothing dimmed his wit.

When Mirza Mehdi Hussain Majrooh enquired about his pension in a letter, he replied:

Miyan be-rizq jeene ka mujhko dhab aa gaya
Iss taraf se khatir jamaa rakhna
Ramzan ka maheena roze khaa khaa kar kataa. Khuda Razzaq hai, kuch aur khaane ko na mila to gham to hai!
Miyan I have got used to living in a state of penury.
Be rest assured from my side.
In the month of Ramzan, I lived by fasting and God is Bounteous and if nothing else, at least there is sorrow.

He died in a state of despair at the age of 73 years. Towards the end he could not hear and people had to write down anything that they wanted to convey to him.

In 1277 AH (1860/61 AD) Mirza Ghalib had fallen sick and written a chronogram for his death 'Ghalib murd [Ghalib died]'.

However, he survived that illness and eventually died in 1869. The present chronogram was written by his student Mir Majruh and included those words.

Nawab Mustafa Ali Khan Shefta (1809–1869 AD)

Shayad issi ka naam hai muhabbat Shefta
Ek aag si hai seene ke andar lagi huyi
Perhaps this is what is called love Shefta
A fire, which is lit inside my chest

Mustafa Ali Khan Shefta

Nawab Mustafa Ali Khan Shefta (1809–1869 AD) was a famous poet and critic. He was a contemporary of Mirza Ghalib. He belonged to the famous Bangash family and was buried in their family graveyard which was very close to the Loharu graveyard. He was a close friend of Mirza Ghalib, who stood by him in his hour of need, and it's fitting that they spend their eternal sleep near each other. Unfortunately, heavy construction in the twentieth century has resulted in many changes and, since no headstone or marker indicates his grave, we don't know which one it is. A relative now in Pakistan told me and of his grave there that this was their family cemetery.

I recited a fatiha for him and for all those buried there.

Atgah Khan's Tomb

Khan Azam Khan sipah Azam Khan
Ke chu ou kas da reen zamana nadeed
Beh-Shahadat raseed mah e Siyam
Sharbat e maut rozeh dar chasheed
Kaash saal e digar shaheed shudi
Ke shudi saal faut Khan e Shaheed.
The great commander Khan Azam Khan soldier Azam Khan
No one has seen such a brave in this era
The month of Ramzan bore witness that
A fasting man tasted the syrup of death
Alas! Had he been martyred some other year
You have died in the same year as Khan e Shaheed

Shamsuddin was the son of Mir Yaar Mohammad of Ghazní, a simple farmer. He entered Prince Kámrán's service as a common soldier and helped him to safety after the battle of Kannauj. Humáyún appointed him to his service and subsequently appointed his wife as a wet nurse (or *anagah*) to Prince Akbar at Amarkot, conferring upon her the title of 'Jí Jí Anagah'. Shamsuddin remained with prince Akbar while Humáyún was in Persia and later received the title

'Atgah Khán' (*atgah* meaning foster father). This family was highly respected in the royal hierarchy.

Akbar had many foster mothers. Adham Khan, son of another foster mother Maham Anga, was jealous of Atgah Khan's influence and position in the court and killed him in a fit of jealousy. On 12th Ramzan 969 AH (1561 AD), when Atgah was sitting in one of the rooms of Diwan e Aam with other nobles, Adham Khan came there with few other men:

> All rose to greet him, when Adham struck Atgah with his dagger, and told one of his companions, to kill him. He then went with the dagger in his hand towards the sleeping apartments of Akbar, who had been awakened by the noise in the state hall. Looking out from a window, he saw what had happened, rushed forward sword in hand, and met Adham on a high archway (aiwán) near the harem. 'Why have you

Atgah Khan's Tomb

> killed my foster father, you son of a bitch?' (bachah i ládah), cried Akbar. 'Stop a moment, Majesty,' replied Adham, seizing Akbar's arms, 'first inquire.' Akbar drew away his hands and struck Adham a blow in the face, which sent him 'spinning' to the ground. 'What are you standing here gaping,' said Akbar to one of his attendants of the name of Farhat Khán, 'bind this man.' This was done, and at Akbar's orders, Adham Khán was twice thrown down from the dais (çuffah) of the Aiwán to the ground, with his head foremost. The corpses of Adham and Atgah were then sent to Dihlí.[57]

Though they were sent at the same time, Adham Khan was buried a day before Atgah Khan. The date of the latter's death was written in two chronograms:

Do khoon shud
Raft az zulm sar e Azam Khan
Two murders have been committed
The cruelty against Azam Khan has been avenged

Mirza Aziz Kokaltash Khan, the son of Atgah Khan, had the tomb built over his father's grave. It's 30 square feet and is 54 feet in height (including the dome). The inscription on the southern doorway is: 'This noble edifice was finished in the year 974 AH (1566–67 AD) under the superintendence of Ustad Khuda Quli.'

Around the arches on all the four sides run Quranic inscriptions, which conclude with a reference to Baqi Mohammad, the scribe.

Dargah of Hazrat Nizamuddin Auliya

Hazrat Nizamuddin Auliya

> *How many scholars and learned men have flourished in the past,*
> *but nobody [now] knows who they were and where they lived.*
> *What really survives is [the memory of] living happily with people.*
> *This is real spiritual living.*
>
> *Hazrat Sheikh Nizamuddin Auliya*[58]

Hazrat Nizamuddin Auliya (1244–1324 AD) is arguably the most famous saint of Delhi. He was born Mohammad bin Ahmed bin Ali Bukhari, earning the titles Sultan-ul-Mashaikh (King of Saints), Nizamuddin Auliya and Mehboob e Ilahi. It is said that during his time, he was referred to simply as Sultanji.

His paternal grandfather was Syed Ali Bukhari and his maternal grandfather was Khwaja Arab, both enlightened and pious men. As first cousins, they had their daughters Khwaja Syed Ahmed and Bibi Zuleikha married. They traced their family tree to Imam Hussain ibn Imam Ali Abu Talib. They were natives of Bukhara who had to leave during the Mongol invasions. The family migrated to India and reached Delhi after time spent in Lahore and Badayun, a thriving centre of Sufism.

His mother Bibi Zuleikha ensured that he was educated well; Maulana Alauddin Usooli Badayuni and Shadi Muqri were two of his teachers.

It is said that Hazrat Nizamuddin Auliya was intelligent, sagacious and blessed with quick understanding. He had finished his education in 'uloom e aqli wa naqli' (or religion and sciences) by the age of fourteen. His teachers gave him the title of 'Maulana Nizamuddin Al Behas' (the controversialist) and 'Mehfil e Shikan' (Destroyer of Arguments).

When the young Nizamuddin finished studying Quduri's books on Muslim jurisprudence, Maulana Usuli declared that he had now qualified for the turban of scholarship or 'dastar e fazilah' (a modern-day convocation). Hazrat Nizamuddin Auliya's mother procured a four-yard piece of cloth from a cotton weaver despite their dire circumstances. As the turban was tied around Nizamuddin's head, he bowed in front of his teacher's feet. Saint Ali Maula from Badayun is said to have pronounced that the boy was destined for greatness on seeing this action.

At sixteen, he migrated with his mother and sister to Delhi. He studied *ilm e hadith* (study of the sayings of the Prophet) under the leading religious scholar of the day, Maulana Kamaluddin Zahid. His companion was Sheikh Najibuddin Mutawakkil, the brother of Baba Farid Ganj e Shakkar. It was said that it was hearing the morning prayers in Jama Masjid and a powerful ayat that made him decide to spend his time in remembrance of Allah:[59]

> *Alam ya'ni lilladhîna 'âmanû an takhsha'a qulûbuhum li dhikri Allah*
> *Is it not time that the hearts of all who have attained to faith should feel humble at the remembrance of God*
>
> *(Quran 57:16)*

He left for Ajodhan and spent time with Baba Farid Ganj e Shakkar, who was then ninety years old. He welcomed Nizamuddin with these words:

Ai aatish e firaqat dilha kabab kardah
Sailab e ishtiaqat jaanha kharab kardah
The fire of your separation has burnt many hearts.
The storm of desire to meet you has ravaged many lives.[60]

At age twenty, Nizamuddin took an oath of allegiance with him. Baba Farid Ganj e Shakkar arranged for a charpoy to be readied for Nizamuddin, who was reluctant to use it as other saints in the *khanqah* always slept on the floor. When asked whether he would obey his master, he decided to obey by overturning the bed to sleep on it. It is believed that he returned from Ajodhan with the words of his master ringing in his ears: 'Make sure that you keep your enemies happy, whatever way you may have to ensure that.' He visited Baba Farid Ganj e Shakkar thrice.

Building of the Khanqah

One who serves becomes the Master

Hazrat Nizamuddin Auliya

Hazrat Nizamuddin Auliya settled finally in Ghiyaspur. While his disciples wanted to build him a *khanqah*, it is said that Hazrat Nizamuddin Auliya refused, saying that anyone who built his khanqah would not survive. Imad-ul-Mulk Ziauddin Vakil was a disciple who accepted this answer with humility, willing to sacrifice his life for the saint's comfort. Hazrat Nizamuddin Auliya told him to ready the khanqah in a month and, during that time, he stayed in Kilokri.

It is said that the disciple spent 400 asharfi to arrange for 'majlis e sema', and that it was during this time that he passed away with his head in the saint's lap.

When Hazrat was living in Ghiyaspur he and his followers faced many hardships with often nothing to eat. When they would go hungry for a few days, his disciples would supplicate for food (zambeel gadagiri) by leaving a scrip at the door and people could put in whatever food they wanted in it.

When Sultan Jalaluddin Khilji heard of this he sent a message that he wanted to present a few villages for the upkeep of the khanqah so that the saint could be free to devote his time in prayers, but Hazrat refused the gift. He stayed away from power and money all his life and put his faith in God. From childhood he had grown up hearing his mother say, 'We are the guests of Allah, tonight,' whenever there was no food in the house.

When Sultan Jalaluddin Khilji insisted on visiting the saint he famously said that a faqeer's house had two doors and if the Sultan entered from one, he would exit from the other.

The Sultan was determined and conveyed his intention to his courtier and the saint's disciple, Hazrat Amir Khusrau. Hazrat Amir Khusrau was caught in a bind but his ultimate loyalty lay with his spiritual master and relayed this message to the saint who immediately left for Ajodhan.

The Sultan was upset that his secret had been let out and Hazrat Amir Khusrau replied that if if the Sultan got angry with him, only his life was in danger but if his Sheikh got angry with him his faith, after life and salvation were threatened. Sultan Jalaluddin Khilji was very pleased by this answer and forgave Hazrat Amir Khusrau.

Once Sultan Alauddin Khilji sent a letter to him via his son Khizr Khan who was a disciple of the saint inviting his suggestions for governance. The saint refused saying.

'We dervishes have nothing to do with the affairs of state. I have settled in a corner away from the men of the city and spend my time in praying for the Sultan and other Muslims. If the Sultan does not like this, let him tell me so. I will go and live elsewhere. God's earth is vast enough.'[61]

The Sultan was very impressed that the saint had no political inclinations and wanted to come and seek his blessings but the saint sent back a message saying that there was no need for the king to come, as he would bless him from afar.

There is another story given in Siyar-ul-Arifeen, which talks of his hardships and how they were ended. An old lady stayed near his khanqah and she had great faith in him. She would earn money from her spinning wheel and her daily diet was a simple bread of barley grain. One day she brought half a kg of flour to the saint as a gift. The saint gave it to his follower Syed Kamaluddin Yaqub to put water in it and put it on the fire to cook. Just as it was cooking when a faqeer, with a blanket covering him, passed by and asked for some food. Hazrat Nizamuddin picked up the pot of flour and offered it to him. The faqeer finished of the hot food and threw the earthern pot on the ground breaking it in pieces. He said that he had been instructed by Sheikh Farid who had given him hidden blessings and so he had broken his external hardships and starvation. From that day onwards there was a constant flow of tributes, gifts, money and treasures and the khanqah never wanted for anything.

However, he would ensure that whatever money or gifts that came to the khanqah were distributed amongst the poor the same day, before the night set in. He wouldonly leave for his Friday prayers after he had had the entire khanqah swept and all money and material things found there, distributed amongst the poor.

Langar Khana

> *You will be the tree under whose soothing shadow the people will find comfort*
>
> *Baba Farid for Hazrat Nizamuddin Auliya*

Thousands of people used to eat at the langar khana in the saint's lifetime. More than 1,500 people eat at the premises during Ramzan.

Jamaat Khana

Chhap tilak sab cheeni re mose naina milaikay
Prem bhati ka madhva pilaikay
Matvali kar leeni re mose naina milaikay
You've stolen my identity with just a glance
You've intoxicated me with a love potion
I'm drunk in love by just a glance from your eyes

Hazrat Amir Khusrau

From the writings of Hazrat Nasiruddin Chiragh Dehli we come to know that when Sema mehfils were held, for Hazrat Nizamuddin Auliya, he would be accompanied by Hazrat Amir Khusrau and Amir Hasan on his right, and Khwaja Mubasshir and his slaves on his left. All three were very skilled at music and singing. Hazrat Amir Khusrau would start the mehfil by singing a ghazal and would repeat the verse, which sent Hazrat Nizamuddin into a trance. Sultan Alauddin had asked his trusted noble named Qambar Beg Turk Sultan who was a devotee of the Sultan-ul-Mashaik to remember and recite to him the verses, which sent the saint into a trance. Once the saint went into a trance after listening to the verses from Hadiqa al Haqiqa (Walled Garden of Truth) of Hakeem Sanai.

Qambar Beg noted down these verses and took them into the presence of the Sultan. The Sultan would read them and rub them against his eyes.

Qambar Beg said, 'Alas! It's very sad that if you have such faith in the Saint why don't you take the opportunity of spending time in his company and being blessed by Him.'

The Sultan replied, 'I am a Sultan but am submerged in evil sins and wrong-doing and I am too ashamed to go near him. You take my sons Khizr Khan and Shadi Khan to him and make them his disciples.'

Qambar Khan took Khizr Khan into the saint's presence along with some (two lakh rupees) monetary tribute from the Sultan. Both the sons took an oath of allegiance with the saint.

The Jamaat Khana Masjid is the oldest surviving building in the Dargah and lies to its west. Firoz Khan Tughlaq mentions in his Futuhat that he built it:

And I constructed a new Jamaat Khanah, which was not there.

But Alauddin Khilji's son Khizr Khan built the mosque itself while Firoz Shah added the side rooms used as women's mosque and langar khana. Its lofty dome is very majestic and can be seen in most iconic photographs of the dargah complex. The middle part is 14 yards and had a golden bowl hanging from the centre. It is still hanging there. It has handsome arches of the Jamaatkhana have the same lotus bud design as Alai Darwaza. The date of his rehlat (leaving the world) is inscribed on a wall in the Mosque.

The administrator (Nizam) of the two worlds, the king of water and earth surely became a lamp for both the worlds
When I sought the date of his death from the invisible, the invisible crier said, 'The Emperor of Religion' (725 AH = 1325 AD)

Astana Sharif

Gori soye sej pe mukh pe dare kes
Chal Khusrau ghar aapne sanjh bhayi chahu des
The fair maiden sleeps on her bed, face covered with her tresses
O Khusrau let's go home, for darkness has spread everywhere

Hazrat Amir Khusaru on the grave of Hazrat Nizamuddin

After a brief illness, Hazrat Nizamuddin Auliya died in 1324 AD on a Wednesday morning. He was eighty-two. Astana Sharif was built next to the Chabutra Yarani (Platform of Friends).

Aastana Sharif / Shrine

Hazrat Nizamuddin Auliya wanted a simple grave but Muhammad bin Tughlaq had a dome built over the shrine and Firoz Shah had repairs done with sandalwood doors and a canopy built (which have since disappeared). The original structure has been added to at various times by devotees and changed considerably over time. In 1562-63 AD, Faridun Khan erected the present building with a bulbous marble dome, decorated with black marble stripes and crowned by a *kalash*. There are four small *burjis* on all four corners of the dargah.

Khalilullah Khan, Umdat-ul-Mulk, the governor of Delhi in 1652 AD, built the verandah around the tomb using red sandstone and marble. The pillars of the verandah were replaced with marble ones in 1808 AD by Nawab Ahmad Baksh of Firozpur. He added a miniature dome on the parapet.

The 6.9 feet wide verandah running all around it has five trefoil-arched doorways supported by twenty marble columns called *bastdari*. A lovely sloping marble *chajja* provides shade to these arches. A parapet with a series of small domes topped by miniature gold finials runs all around the tomb. Khurshid Jah of Hyderabad gifted the marble balustrade that surrounds the shrine proper.

The 18 square feet shrine is enclosed by marble jalis, which are supported by beautiful yellow panels decorated with green and red. Peerzada Altamash Nizami, a direct descendant of Hazrat Nizamuddin Auliya and a trustee at the dargah, told me that a Kashmiri devotee of the saint did the renovation work, which explains the lacquered finish of the shrine. It resembles a Kashmiri papermache decoration.

The entrance door to the shrine is on the southern side. There is a canopy over the actual grave at all times.

Dargah of Hazrat Amir Khusrau

Khabaram raseed imshab ki nigaar khwahi aamad
Sar-e man fidaa-e raah-e ki sawaar khwahi aamad
Tonight I received news that you, O beloved, would come
May my head be sacrificed to the road along which you will come riding
Hazrat Amir Khusrau

Hazrat Amir Khusrau was born as Abul Hasan Yameenuddin in Patiali, Etah, in 1253 AD. He was the son of a Turkish soldier, Amir Saifuddin Turk Lachin Mahmood from Balkh, and a Rajput woman. His maternal grandfather Imad-ul-Mulk Rawat Arz was minister in Balban. His father took him to Hazrat Nizamuddin Auliya when he was eight years old.

The young Amir Khusrau is said to have told his father that he would select his spiritual guide himself, composing this verse while waiting for Hazrat Nizamuddin Auliya:

Dargah of Hazrat Amir Khusrau

Tu-an Shah e ke bar aiwan e qasrat
Kabutar gar nashinad baz garded
Gharib-e mustanande baradar amad
Be ayat andar un ya baz gardad
You are such a mighty King
that if a pigeon sits on your palace, it turns into a hawk.
An outsider and a needy person has come at your door,
please let him know whether he should come in, or go away.

Hazrat Nizamuddin Auliya sent him the following reply:

Biya yet andarun marde haqiqat,
Kibama yak nafas hamraz gardad,
Agar ablah buwad an mard nadan,
Azan rahe ki amad baz gardad.
The person who knows the truth may come inside

so that we may exchange divine secrets between us for a moment.
If that person is ignorant, then he should return
on the same path from where he has come here

It was said that this is when the two became inseparable. Hazrat Nizamuddin Auliya called Hazrat Amir Khusrau 'Miftah-al Sama' (or the Key of Religious Ecstasy). According to legend, Hazrat Nizamuddin Auliya rubbed his 'luab e dahan' (saliva) on his disciple's lips to make his words and voice even sweeter.

He recited the verse:

Zulfat za-har-do jaanib, khoonrez e aashiqaan ast
Cheezey namii tawaaN guft, roo e tu darmeyaan ast
While your tresses shed lovers' blood from both sides
Your face, in the middle, robs them of any power to complain
(translated by Avinash Pandey)

As a result of this, he received the title of Tuti e Hind (Parrot of India). There were poets in the reign of Sultan Alauddin Khilji as had never existed before and never appeared since. The incomparable Hazrat Amir Khusrau stands unequalled for the volume of his writings and the originality of his ideals; for, while other great masters of prose and verse have excelled in one or two branches, Hazrat Amir Khusrau was conspicuous in every department of letters. A man with such mastery over all forms of poetry has never existed in the past and may, perhaps, not come into existence before the Day of Judgement. In addition to his wit and talent, he was an advanced mystic. He fasted every day and passed most of his time in reading the Quran and in obligatory and supererogatory prayers. He excelled in the playing and composition of music. Almighty God had bestowed on him all the qualities that appertain to an artisitic and cultured mind.

Hazrat Amir Khusrau was a superb musician in his own right, credited with the invention of several musical instruments, including the tabla, and with laying the theoretical basis for much of Indo-Muslim music. The lilt and melody he introduced to the ghazal is said to persist even today.[62]

In fact, no one after him has been able to obtain the title of 'naik', which was the highest title bestowed on a musician. Hazrat Amir Khusrau is credited with turning the *sema* music into qawwali as it is sung today. He was entrusted with the work of developing the qawwali as a complete form of music and he selected twelve young students, whom he called 'qawwal bachcha', to present the Qual Qalbana. He is also credited with genres such as the *tarana, khayal* and the *qual*. He is also said to have composed numerous new ragas as such *yaman kalyan*, *sazgiri* and *sarparda*. He was credited with the creation of seventeen talas (patterns of rhythm), such as *teen* tal, *jhoomra* and *ara chautala*. He is said to have created six forms of music, namely Qual, Qalbana, Khayal, Tarana, Naqsh and Gul. The last two have lapsed into obscurity but the rest remain. The word 'tarana' itself means a 'song' in Persian.

Munshi Raziuddin and his sons, Farid Ayaz and Abu Mohammad, are descendants from the same qawwal bachchas. By his time, Indian music was disappearing because of Persian influence. It is believed that he gave Indian music a new lease on life. Khusrau was already a part of Indo-Iranian music. Hazrat Amir Khusrau was also instrumental for the language we know as Hindustani. He bridged the gap in the courts of the Delhi Sultanate where nobles spoke Persian and Turkish while the locals spoke Khari Boli and Brij Bhasha. He did so by writing dohas, riddles, and songs for every occasion in what was known as 'Hindavi', which went on to become Hindustani. Hazrat Amir Khusrau has ninety-two literary works to his credit and innumerous verses.

Sultan Jalauddin Khilji, who was a great admirier of Hazrat Amir Khusrau, gave him the highest status he attained in his life: Keeper of the Holy Quran. He was even appointed the chief courtier. He continued as poet laureate under Sultan Alauddin Khilji, during which period he was most prolific. As a fervent devotee of Hazrat Nizamuddin Auliya, it is said that Hazrat Amir Khusrau was devastated when the saint passed away and wrote this doha:

Gori soye sej par mukh par dare kes
Chal Khusrau ghar aapnay saanjh bhayi chahu des
The fair maiden rests on the wreath (of roses),
Her tresses covering her face,
Let us, Oh Khusrau, go back now,
The dark dusk settles in four corners

Though he was consoled by everyone especially Hazrat Nasiruddin Chiragh Delhi, he was inconsolable. He spent his time weeping at the foot of his Master's shrine within six months he passed away at the age of 74 on a Friday 20th Zil Qayda 725 AH (1324 AD). Their love for each other had been so great that Mehboob e Ilahi had said that Amir should be buried near him, as they could not share a grave as per Islam and so he was buried on the Yaarani Chabutra next to his master, Hazrat Nizamuddin Auliya.

Basheeruddin Ahmad writes that there had been a space left next to the right of Hazrat Nizamuddin's own grave but some Khwaja Sara said that if the two graves were next to each other, people who came to pay respects might get confused. Thus he was buried a little away in a separate tomb. It seems that the Khwaja Sara who had thus flouted the saint's will died in his sleep a few days later. For ages his grave was without a dome or enclosure and it was built much later in 1014 AH/1605 AD. In the last years of Akbar and initial years of Jahangir's reign, Imaduddin Hasan, known as Tahir, constructed an enclosure and a beautiful marble dome on his grave and got this verse inscribed on it:

Ai Khusrau benazeer e aalam
Beh rauza tu mora niyaaz ast
Oh matchless Khusrau
I have faith in your shrine

There are red sandstone screens around the dome and on the south arches have been added on which a roof has been made. In the outer enclosure to the south is buried Shamsuddin Mahru, the son of Amir Khusrau's sister.

Chabutra Yarani

Nami danam chi manzil bood shab jaay ki man boodam;
Baharsu raqs-e bismil bood shab jaay ki man boodam
I wonder what was the place where I was last night,
All around me were half-slaughtered victims of love,
tossing about in agony

Hazrat Amir Khusrau

This was the platform on which Hazrat Nizamuddin Auliya used to sit with his friends, giving sermons and discourses. It now houses the graves of important personages, including Hazrat Amir Khusrau. Another is Maulana Alauddin Nili (1360 AD), the khalifa of Hazrat Nizamuddin Auliya's legacy in the *khanqah*. The descendants of that family are still caretakers of the dargah. In front of Hazrat Amir Khusrau's shrine are graves of two of the most famous historians of the fourteenth century: Ziauddin Barani and Shams Siraj Afif. They were both disciples of the saint. A son of Hazrat Amir Khusrau, Amir Haji, is also buried there.

Tomb of Princess Jahanara

While mankind remains mere baggage in the world
It will be swept along, as in a boat, asleep.
What can they see in sleep?
What real merit or punishment can there be?

Hakim Sanai Ghaznavi

Tomb of Princess Jahanara

Princess Jahanara (1614–1681 AD) was the eldest and favourite daughter of Emperor Shah Jahan. She lived through the most glorious era of the Mughal empire. She earned the titles of Sahibat al-Zamani (Lady of the Age), Padishah Begum (Lady Emperor) and Begum Saheb (Princess of Princesses). She was so powerful that she was given her own palace outside the confines of the Agra Fort. She aligned with Dara Shukoh in the battle of succession and gave up her pre-eminent position in the court after Emperor Aurangzeb's victory, retiring to look after her father in Agra Fort.

She regained her position in court after Emperor Shah Jahan's death, reconciling with Emperor Aurangzeb. Princess Jahanara was a disciple of Mullah Shah Badakhshi, who initiated her into the Qadiriyya Sufi order in 1641 AD. While he would have liked to have appointed as her his successor, rules of the Qadiriyya order did not allow it. She died in 1681 AD and is buried in a simple marble enclosure in the dargah of Hazrat Nizamuddin Auliya, in a structure built during her lifetime. This tomb is ornamented with embossed traceries.

Stephen Carr wrote in 1876 AD that this structure is 'is hollow at the top and exposed to the sky – the hollow is filled with earth covered with green grass'. Today, it is covered with rose petals and flowers. The grave is an enclosure of four walls, about 16 inches by 12 inches and over 8 inches high. Each of the walls consists of three panels covered with marble screens of lattice work. The wall with the door has two panels, with the door taking place of the third screen. The top of the walls had a perforated marble balustrade but only a small piece of it exists today. There are four small marble minarets on the four corners of the enclosure.

Princess Jahanara's grave is flanked by the grave of Mirza Nili (the son of Shah Alam) on the right and Jamal-un-Nisa, the daughter of Emperor Akbar II, on the left near the langar khana of the dargah. The grave is considered to have magical properties today and mentally disturbed women are brought and left here. It is a disturbing thought because this is done against their will sometimes, when they should instead be given clinical treatment.

Princess Jahanara inherited half of her mother Mumtaz Mahal's property. She wanted to distribute it all amongst the *khadims* of the dargah but Emperor Aurangzeb did not permit it. Sir Syed, describing this enclosure, wrote, 'This *muhajjar* is a piece of Noor (light) and I would not be very far wrong if I called it Manzil e Maah (destination of the Moon) because Mahpara (a piece of the moon) is sleeping here. I can also call it the Makan e Noor (House of Light) because it is the resting place of a Khurshid Talat (one whose countenance is like the Sun).' A tablet in the enclosure has a beautiful couplet that Princess Jahanara wrote herself:

Huwal Hayyul Al Qayyum
Baghair subza na poshad kase mazaar mara
Ki qabr posh ghariban hamin gayah bas-ast
Al faqira, Al faaniya Jahanara mureed
Khajgaana Chist, Bint e Shah Jahan
Badshah Ghazi Anar Allah Barhana

1681 AD

He is the Living, the Sustaining
There cannot be any other curtain of my tomb except the humble covering of grass. Grass alone is sufficient to cover the grave of a poor person, as I am a Disciple of the Khwaja Moin-ud-Din Chishti, Daughter of Shah Jahan the Conqueror, May Allah illuminate his proof.

Tomb of Emperor Muhammad Shah

Uss jangal mein aah Nazeer ek tinka aan na jhaankega
Sab thaath pada rah jaavega jab laad chalega banjara
No one will even cast a second glance at that jungle
Everything will be left in the world when, death takes you with it
Nazeer Akbarabadi

Nasiruddin Muhammad Shah was a Mughal emperor between 1719 and 1748 AD. His reign saw tumultuous times with rebellion all over his territory.

Tomb of Emperor Mohammad Shah

Nadir Shah attacked and sacked Delhi during this time. Despite this, his reign was the zenith of Delhi's cultural existence.

The tomb is elegant with tasteful design, beautifully decorated with inlay and stone carvings. Its once pearly white marble sheen is now yellow and neglected. The enclosure of the tomb has an intricately sculpted marble door, with sides carved from pieces of marble. The tomb also contains the graves of the emperor's wife Nawab Saheba Mahal, his grandson Mirza Jigar and the graves of other princes of the royal family.

According to a now-famous anecdote, a Sufi fakir once told Bahadur Shah Zafar that the destruction of the Mughal empire was ordained when Emperor Muhammad Shah built his grave between the shrines of Hazrat Nizamuddin Auliya and Hazrat Amir Khusrau. It is said that Muhammad Shah bought the land from the *khadims* of the dargah at a price of one lakh rupees and built this enclosure himself. Peerzada Altamash Nizami told me a story that Emperor Muhammad Shah tricked the *khadims* by holding them captive at a dinner he invited them to, until they agreed to give him the land of the dargah.

Tomb of Mirza Jahangir

Ai Jahangir apna adl to dekh
Koi bhar kar yahan se aah utha
O Jahangir such is the state of your justice
That someone just left from here with a sigh

Swaleh Nadeem

This enclosure is very similar to the enclosure of Muhammad Shah Badshah and was meant to be a copy of it, however that was not achieved, as the marble wasn't as pure and flawless. Despite this, once upon a time it must have been very beautiful. Today there is a desolate feeling here and people use it as a shortcut to and from the dargah.

Mirza Jahangir, the son and heir of Akbar Shah II was exiled to Allahabad and put under house arrest by the British for taking a potshot at the British resident Sir Archibald Seton in 1808. He died there in 1821 AD.

His mother, Nawab Mumtaz Mahal who loved him greatly, got his body brought back to Delhi and buried here. For some strange reason his grave has a *takhti*, which denotes the grave of a female and not qalam on it. Maybe as he was persona non grata for the British Government this was done deliberately. His brother Mirza Babar is also buried in the same enclosure.

The prince remains forgotten and his neglected grave enclosure is just a convenient point for entering the dargah and avoiding the crowd of devotees, for those who know this shortcut.

Baoli of Hazrat Nizamuddin Auliya's Dargah

Ashk e nadaamat ke saamne
Aab e zamzam be-maa'ni
The tears of repentance
Are more precious than Aab e zamzam

Sunil Kumar Jashn

Situated at the back of the dargah in a separate enclosure, the story of this *baoli* is a famous one. It was completed in 1321 AD. It is said that Hazrat Nizamuddin Auliya blessed the *baoli*, declaring that its water will benefit all mankind. The water from it is said to be holy and people come here to bathe to get rid of spirits and diseases.

The *baoli* measures 180 feet by 120 feet and is enclosed by walls on three sides. Steps descend into it from the north, going all the way to the bottom. There are broader steps at points for sitting and resting.

In 1379 AD, houses were built on the southern side of the *baoli* during the reign of Sultan Firoz Shah. Children now jump into the *baoli* from the roofs and it is said Mohammad Maaruf Ibn Wahiduddin built some houses on the southern side of this *baoli* during the reign of Sultan Firoz Shah.

There were niches built into the walls of the *baoli* where men and women could stand and bathe but these are partially covered by the water. According to Sir Syed, 'The water level is very near the surface and ignorant people have a bath in this thinking that the water has healing powers. People make *mannats* here to get rid of jinns and evil spirits and women pray for pregnancy.'

There are remains of two old *gumbads* from the Pathan era on the southern side of the *baoli* of which little is known. Sir Syed wrote: 'There is a marble *burj* to the west with a beautiful marble tomb inside. The ninety-nine names of Allah and Quranic ayat are inscribed on it. I have not seen such beautiful calligraphy elsewhere. The year is inscribed on it but due to some error by the inscriber it is difficult to figure out whether it's 1008 or 1080 AH. However, the verse inscribed there rhymes with 1080.'

This structure was encroached upon by a family living next door who closed the structure with bricks and made a toilet in front of it, thus blocking the view of the *baoli*. The toilet has been dismantled and the monument is currently under restoration by the Aga Khan Trust for Culture. The name of the lady buried inside it is known as Bai Kodak Dai.

According to Syed Farid Nizami, this pavilion was probably the point where the palanquins of the Mughal princesses were set down, since there is a direct path to the dargah from here. Emperor Muhammad Shah had a vaulted roof built for devotees to cover the passage from the masjid to the *baoli*.

Hazrat Khwaja Taqiuddin Nuh ka Mazar

The tomb of Khwaja Taqiuddin Nuh, son of Hazrat Nizamuddin Auliya's sister, Bibi Jannat, is outside the premises of the dargah. It's a simple grave.

Celebrations of Basant in the Dargah

Sakal ban phool rahi sarson,
Umbva boray, tesu phulay,
Koyal bolay daar daar,
Aur gori karat singaar,
Malaniyan gadhwa lay aayin karson
Every field is filled with yellow mustard blooms
Mango buds open, flame of the forest trees blossom,
Every branch echoes with the koel's call
The lovely maiden dons her make up
The garden ladies bring fragrant bouquets

These Purbi lyrics sung in the melody of Raag Bahar herald the beginnings of the celebrations at the dargah of Hazrat Nizamuddin Auliya on the eve of Basant Panchami. Peerzada Altamash Nizami told me that the celebrations in the dargah go back to the death of Khwaja Taqiuddin Nuh. Hazrat Nizamuddin

Auliya is said to have been deeply attached to his nephew and his loss was a deep blow.

Hazrat Amir Khusrau made many efforts to make the saint smile again. He is said to have seen a group of women from the village, dressed in yellow and carrying mustard flowers, singing on the road to the *khanqah*. He asked them whether this made their God happy and when the women told him it did, he is said to have dressed in a yellow sari and sung the song, '*Sakal ban phool rahi sarson*'. Hazrat Nizamuddin Auliya rejoiced with his favourite disciple and, after this day, it became a tradition at the dargah.

I have attended these celebrations in the past few years and the atmosphere is euphoric. A langar is held in the dargah complex and various qawwali groups sing in the courtyard. The qawwal singers gather in a lane opposite Mirza Ghalib's grave after the afternoon prayers or *asr*. After a ceremonial prayer, the procession commences singing. The young and the old, everybody joins the procession into the Nizamuddin basti and enter the dargah via the grave of Khwaja Taqiuddin Nuh.

Once in the dargah, the attendees who are part of the procession hold a yellow sheet over their heads and enter the shrine. This is the only occasion in which singing of the qawwali happens inside the shrine. During my visit, there was great rejoicing with qawwalis and music and the celebrations usually last a few hours. There is a final visit to make offerings at the grave of Hazrat Amir Khusrau. The courtyard of the shrine on the eve of spring is full of people dressed in yellow from all areas, regions and faiths, united in a common love for the people's saint.

Aaj Basant Manaley Suhangan
Aaj Basant Manaley
Anjan Manjan Kar Piya
Lambay Neher Lagaaye
Tu Kya Sovay Neend Maasi

So Jaagay Teray Bhaag, Suhagan
Aaj Basant Manalay
Rejoice, oh loved one, rejoice,
Spring is here, rejoice.
Don your make-up, put kohl on your eyes,
Braid your long tresses,
Oh, wake up from your sleep,
Your destiny too has woken up
It's spring here, rejoice.

Urs of a Saint

Urs (from Arabic literally 'wedding') is the death anniversary of a Sufi saint in South Asia and is usually held at the saint's dargah (shrine or tomb). The concept of death as an 'Urs' or a wedding anniversary has been taken from the Hadith: 'Sleep just like the bride.' (*Mishkhat, a book of hadith*)

The Angels say to the pious in the grave, 'Sleep with restfulness and comfort, just like a bride.'

In Sufi philosophy, the Beloved is God or the Divine. The person seeking oneness with God is the lover. This is *ishq e haqeeqi*, which literally means 'the real love' but metaphorically it means 'the love of God'. It refers to the belief that only God is worth loving and He is the only one who can return His creatures' love for Him.

Khusrau darya prem ka, ulti wa ki dhaar,
Jo utra so doob gaya, jo dooba so paar.
Oh Khusrau, the river of love
Runs in strange directions.
One who jumps into it drowns,
And one who drowns, gets across.

The death of a Sufi saint, therefore, is regarded as *wisaal* (union with the beloved) and the death anniversary is celebrated as a wedding anniversary, not as an occasion for mourning.

Yeh duniya mere babul ka ghar, woh duniya sasural
The material world is considered to be the parents house while the afterlife is the house of the beloved.

Dargah Hazrat Inayat Shah

Ek khalish hoti hai mehsoos rag o jaan ke qareeb
Aa'n pahunche hai magar manzil e jaana'n ke qareeb
A strange pain near my jugular vein I can feel
I have reached my destination, near my Beloved

Hasrat Mohani

Hazrat Inayat Shah (1882–1927 AD) was a Sufi preacher of the Chisti silsila. He was a brilliant musician trained in Hindustani music. At the request of his teacher, Sayyed Mohammad Abu Hashim Madani, he travelled west in 1910.

Hazrat Inayat Shah established the Sufi order in 1914 and taught 'universal Sufism', which became the International Sufi Movement in 1923. Sufism, according to him, is based on 'Tauheed' or 'One God' and a unity of religious ideals, love and harmony. This attracted many disciples and he eventually settled in a suburb of Paris called Suresnes. He returned to India in 1926 and passed away in 1927.

Shah was buried in a grave in the dargah of Hazrat Nizamuddin Auliya, on land given to him by a descendant of the saint, Khwaja Hasan Nizami. A *sema mehfil* is held at the dargah every Friday as a tribute to the musician. It is a serene environment and now it is the office of the International Sufi Movement.

It is said that Inayat Shah was a descendant of Tipu Sultan from his maternal side and his daughter, Noor Inayat Shah, was a spy in the second World War as part of the Allied Special Operations.

We were not able to obtain permission to photograph it.

Tomb of Khan e Jahan Tilangani

Kuchh na tha mere paas khone ko
Tum mile ho to dar gaya hu'n main
I had nothing to lose
After meeting you, I am scared

Nomaan Shauque

This tomb of Khan e Jahan Tilangani is in Nizamuddin basti. Khan e Jahan Tilangani was a prime minister in the court of Sultan Firoz Shah. The tomb was the first octagonal one in Delhi, probably built alongside the Kali Masjid in 1370 AD. The tomb is now surrounded by residential houses and it is difficult to visit or photograph it.

Kali Masjid, Hazrat Nizamuddin Basti

Kali Masjid, Hazrat Nizamuddin Basti

Mandir gaye, masjid gaye, piro'n faqiro'n se mile
Ek usko paane ke liye kya kya kiya, kya kya huwa
I visited temples, frequented mosques, met saints and mendicants
I did so much and went through so much just to find Him

Bashir Badr

Originally known as Sanjar Masjid, it acquired the name 'kali' (a corruption of the word 'kalan' which means big) along the way.[63] Built by Junan Khan, it is part of seven mosques built in the era of Sultan Firoz Shah. It still functions under the Delhi Waqf Board.

The trustees of the mosque do not encourage visits, especially by women. It is built in a style similar to Kalan Masjid near Turkman Gate.

IX
Aliganj

Shah e Marda'n

Tomb of Nawab Mirza Najaf Khan

> *The wilayat (domain) of gnosis and faith can suffer decay. The wilayat of compassion can not.*
>
> *Hazrat Nizamuddin Auliya*

Nawab Zulfiqar-ud-Daula Mirza Najaf Khan (1723–1781) was a Persian from the Safavid family who came to India in around 1740. He held the post of Deputy Wazir of Awadh. He was made the commander-in-chief of the Mughal army in 1772 and held the post till his death. Though his tomb is very simple, constructed of stone and lime mortar, he was an important noble of his era. Under him, the Mughal army retained some semblance of glory.

Tomb of Nawab Mirza Najaf Khan

Shah e Mardan Shrine

Shah e Mardan

Kya faiz Ali ke qadam paak se hai
Rauza ki zameen buland aflak se hai
Banta hai wahan durr e Najaf qatra e aab
Paani ki aabru bhi issi khaak se hai
What blessings emanate from Ali's footprint
This shrine is elevated beyond the sky
Here even the pearls of Najaf become drops of water
Even the water's pride springs from being mixed in its dust

Hazrat Ali was the cousin and son-in-law of the Prophet and his chosen successor. It is believed that the Prophet said:

Man Kunto Maula
Fa hada Aliyun Maula
For those whom I am Maula
Ali is also a Maula

The word 'maula' is interpreted by Shias as 'leader', whereas others translate it as 'friend'. Known as the epitome of knowledge and wisdom, he was given the title 'Shah e Mardan' or the 'king of men', so dargahs devoted to him are known as such. This dargah was built by the Shia wife of Emperor Muhamamd Shah, Udham Bai, in the reign of her son Emperor Ahmed Shah Bahadur. She is said to have acquired a stone in 1724 AD with the footstep of Hazrat Ali and had it fixed inside a marble tank. She had a compound wall, assembly hall, *hauz* and mosque built under the supervision of Nawab Javed Khan Khwajasara in 1768 AD.

Burj Kasa e Hazrat Fatima/Bibi ki Chakki

> *Do not let your difficulties fill you with anxiety, after all it is only in the darkest nights that stars shine more brightly.*
>
> *Hazrat Ali ibn Abu Talib*

Next to the Qadam Sharif or 'footmark' is another shrine called Bibi ki Chakki. It is said to be the millstone used by Bibi Fatima, the daughter of the Prophet and Hazrat Ali's wife. It was earlier called Bibi ka Kasa (cup). However, the *kasa* has since been lost, so now it has been renamed Bibi ki Chakki.

I often go there to pray. There is another shrine next to it that is dedicated to Imam Musa Kazim. In 1808, Ishrat Ali Khan got an assembly hall built.

This dargah once spread to as far as Sardarjung's tomb and it is said that the Nawab's body was kept in the dargah while the tomb was built. The huge darwaza at the entrance is called Naqqar Khana. It is plastered a simple white now but is said to have had floral decoration. There is a beautiful white three-domed mosque with a three-arched facade. It is 25 feet by 10 feet. Basheeruddin Ahmad tells us of many old graves under the floor of the courtyard. He says there was also a well and a *baoli* with steps, which today no longer exists.

Dargah Hazrat Arif Ali Shah

Dargah Hazrat Arif Ali Shah

Umr guzri hai isi dasht ki sayyahi main paanchvi pusht hai Shabbir ki maddahi main
I've spent a lifetime traversing this desert with veneration
in Shabbir's service I am the fifth generation

Mir Anees

In the seventeenth century, a Shia man called Syed Arif Ali Shah alias Chatte batte was fleeing from persecution, since he was being pursued by the army. Tired of running, he stopped to rest in Aliganj and invoked Hazrat Ali:

Ya Ali madad
O Ali help me

Legend says that he prayed so much that he became like a two-year-old child. The army came upon him to find a small child and moved on. When Arif Ali Shah came back to his normal size, he saw a footprint of his saviour in front of him. It is said that this is the exact spot where this dargah was built by Syed Arif Ali Shah in 1661 AD. It is believed that the dargah encases this footprint. Cloth fans hanging over the tomb are responsible for the name 'chatte batte'. Qudsia Begum, the wife of Emperor Muhammad Shah, had the structure rebuilt, along with mosques in the compound. Most people wrongly attribute the establishment of the Dargah itself to Qudsia Begum but that is inaccurate.

Basheeruddin Ahmad says the compound walls bore resemblance to the walls of Shahjahanabad, 17 feet high with three darwazas and staircases. This is now in the posh locality of Jor Bagh.

Karbala

Jab qata ki masafat e shab aaftab ne
Jalwa kiya sahar ke rukhe be-hijaab ne
Dekha su e falak Shah e gardoon rakaab ne
MuD kar sada rafeeqo'n ko di us janaab ne
Aakhir hai raat hamd o sana e Khuda karo
Utho fareeza e sahri ko ada karo
When the sun had competed its nightly journey
The unveiled dawn appeared in all its radiance
The king (Husain) whose stirrups are the firmaments looked towards the sky
The Lord turning to his companions, called out to them and said;
At last the time has come; Praise and magnify God
Arise and perform the morning prayer

Mir Anees (translated by Prof C.M. Naim)

Nearby is another enclosure called the Karbala after the battlefield and burial place of Hazrat Ali's son Imam Hussain in Iraq, who was martyred there along with his friends and family.

Karbalas in India are now a generic name for Shia cemeteries and the place where taziya processions end on 10th Muharrum. This place is one of the oldest Shia burial places in the city too.

At the entrance of the Karbala is a unique mosque. The only built structure there is a mehrab wall. It is called the Qanaati Masjid (mosque of the awning) after the permanent awning used to provide shelter to the worshippers. This is dated as being late Mughal period. It is said to have had underground chambers that are now inaccessible. It was built of rubble masonry but like many buildings in Delhi and elsewhere has been plastered and painted over. A wealthy nobleman Captain Ashraf Beg Khan built the compound wall in the later Mughal era. The Darwaza already existed. Though now in a very dilapidated state it must have been quite a grand structure.

The only other significant grave is of Justice Murtaza Fazle Ali. There are some random graves but today all burial there has been stopped. Today the Karbala is a site of ongoing land dispute between the Karbala authorities and a nursery, which has been set up there. It has seen many protests between owners of Rajdhani Nursery and Anjuman e Haideri (the Dargah trust) and local Shias. Today there is a police guard permanently stationed and entry is restricted.

This is the place where all the taziayas are brought during Moharrum for burial. There are many graves in this compound.

Mah Khanum's Tomb

Khusrau baazi prem ki main khelun pi ke sang,
Jeet gayi to piya moray, haari, pi kay sang.
I play the game of love with my beloved,
If I win, the beloved is mine, if I lose, my Beloved I am yours.

Hazrat Amir Khusrau

There is a large cemented platform near the entrance with four steps ascending to it. It used to be 831 feet by 44 feet and 3.5 feet high. A *chabutra* stands next to it, as well as a pavilion with a small doorway which is 6 feet by 3 feet made of *sang e bassi*. A small domed room of 18 feet by 11.5 feet leads into the basement via fourteen steps. This has only a single entrance. The basement is 13.5 square feet with ventilation. There is a single grave in the centre of this room with an elegant headstone telling us that the woman buried there is Mah Khanum. The date is 1762 AD.

Basheeruddin Ahmad says that it is possible she was an important personage from the family of Ashraf Beg Khan. Today we have no knowledge of the identity of a person whose tomb must have been built at great expense and labour. Death is indeed a great leveller!

Tomb of Safdar Jung

Dar o deewar pe hasrat se nazar karte hain
Khush raho ahl e watan hum to safar karte hain
A yearning glance I cast at these walls and doors
God bless you my countrymen for I leave now

Nawab Wajid Ali Shah

This tomb was built for Mirza Muqim Abul Mansur Khan, popularly known as Safdar Jung, by his son Nawab Shuja-ud-Daula in 1754 AD. Safdar Jung was the chief minister in the court of Emperor Ahmed Shah, succeeding his father later as the second Nawab of Awadh. The locals still refer to the tomb as 'Mansur ka maqbara'. The architect was Shaidi Bilal Mohammad Khan and it was built at a cost of three lakh rupees.

The gateway stands on a busy road in Delhi, one of the prettiest in the city. It leads to a domed chamber and has apartments on either side on the upper and lower storeys. A door on the right side leads to the mosque, which is used every Friday for congregational prayers.

Inside Safdar Jung's Tomb

This gateway is a favourite of photographers, who use the arched entrance to the the tomb to make a dramatic frame. This is also a paradisical tomb, standing in the middle of an extensive garden, inspired by Emperor Humayun's tomb. It is the last monumental tomb built under the Mughals. There used to be canals and tanks on all sides but now we just have British lawns. The mausoleum stands on a high platform containing a series of recessed arches. The four facades of the tomb are similar, with engrailed entrance arches in marble and red sandstone and white spandrels. Above the arches, the facade of the central doorway rises above the level of the roof with a set of marble cupolas flanked by a tapering minaret on either side.

The marble dome rises from a sixteen-sided red sandstone drum and follows the Persian bulbous pattern. It is topped by an elegant lotus finial with a marble pinnacle.

The central chamber contains a beautiful marble sarcophagus while the actual grave is in the basement below. There is one more earthen mound in the basement, which is said to be the grave of Safdar Jung's wife, Khujista Banu Begum.

There are eight chambers with attractive designs on the ceilings. These are often havens for young couples spending time together.

There are attractive buildings built on three sides of the garden; the one on the south is called Moti Mahal, the one on the west is called Junglee Mahal and the elegant and beautiful building on the north is known as Badshah Pasand. Till a few years ago, the ASI had its Delhi circle office in Moti Mahal which has since shifted to a government building. Though this is a very popular monument and praised for its beauty, it faced much criticism for its look and construction in the nineteenth and twentieth centuries. Bishop Hebber said that the use of fawn and red sandstone gives it the appearance of 'potted meat'!

The builders were also accused of plundering stones from the tomb of Abdur Rahim Khan e Khana'n for its construction, since disproved by Sir Syed. It is a lovely reminder of a period when the Mughal empire was on the wane but had not quite been written off.

Tomb of Safdar Jung

X

Bagh e Jadd

Masjid and Gumbad, Khairpur (Courtesy: ASI archives)

Lodi Garden, Khairpur

Barso'n raha jinke sar par chatr e zarrin
Turbat pe inke shamiana dekha
Those whose heads for years were covered by golden canopies
I saw lying in graves covered by a simple tent

The Khairpur tombs derive their name from the area, which used to be known as Khairpur district. The four tombs in this area are now on the road between Safdar Jung's tomb and the dargah of Hazrat Nizamuddin Auliya.

Athpula

Tomb of Sultan Mohammad Shah

Tomb of Sultan Muhammad Shah

Tooti hai meri neend magar tumko is se kya?
Bajtey rahein hawaon sey darr, tumko is se kya?
I woke up from sleep, what matter it to you?
The wind knocking on my doors, what matters it to you?
Parvin Shakir

The first one is the tomb of the third king of the Saiyyid dynasty, Sultan Mohammad Shah, the son Farid Khan bin Khizr Khan, who ruled Delhi from 1443–1445 AD. His son, Alauddin Alam Shah, built this tomb. It is built of lime and stone. His son was eventually overthrown by Sultan Bahlol Khan Lodi. The tomb, is known locally as Mubarak Khan ka Gumbad.

It's an octagonal tomb whose dome springs from a sixteen-side drum. The galleries around the tomb and the cupolas on top are very attractive.

The columns, which are at the angles of the arcade, are buttressed; the pendentive of the small domes above the arcade are similar to those in the tomb of Sultan Iltutmish and in the Alai Darwaza. Round the interior of the main dome is a cornice, decorated in a manner which indicates the style of the former decoration of the whole of the interior of the mausoleum.

Its internal diameter is 35 feet and there are sixteen niches built in ceiling of the dome, out of which four are open and the rest closed. 'Allah' was written on each side of these niches.

The *ayat ul kursi*, or verse of the throne, is written in white letters in the topmost part of the ceiling under the dome. There are three other Quranic ayat from 28th Surah of the Quran inscribed in the bigger diameter of the dome along with the ninety-nine names of Allah.

There are many graves inside the tomb but the identity of those buried in them is not known, as they had all been plastered anew with cement. Basheeruddin Ahmad mentions the plastering of the graves but not the year, so it must be post British coming to power in Delhi. No inscription was left on any of the graves. To the north of Muhammad Shah's tomb, Basheeruddin Ahmad mentions an exquisite three-arched masjid with a well near it for ablutions. There are no traces of it to be found today.

Masjid and Gumbad Khairpur

In studying ourselves
We find the harmony
That is our total existence
We do not make harmony
We do not achieve it
Or gain it
It is there - all the time

Taizan Maezumi Roshi

A structure called Bada Gumbad, known as such for its lofty dome, stands here. Dating back to 1494 AD, it has features of Lodi architecture, suggesting that it was probably built around the time of Sultan Sikandar Lodi.

Masjid and Gumbad Khairpur

There are few mosques as attractive as this from the Lodi period. Architecturally, this *gumbad* assumes great importance as it marks a considerable advance in architecture, with the lotus finial on domes reaching their culmination in the Mughal period. This is probably the first single-aisle mosque in Delhi, followed by the Moth ki Masjid and the mosque of Jamali Kamali. We see beautiful incisive plaster work done on its facade along with calligraphy.

It has five arches, with the central one being bigger and well decorated. There are three domes on the mosque with the *kalash* having broken down. There are merlons on the roof parapets. Beglar feels that this mosque must have been exquisitely painted from the inside but this work was painted over by the villagers.

The *gumbad* seems to be the entrance of this mosque. It is 41 feet in diameter from inside and 45 feet from outside. It has a height of 55 feet. The *gumbad* has four entrances. Though now we enter from any side, its actual entrance was to the north which had a staircase of eleven steps on either side. There are eight windows in the dome for ventilation with sixteen niches above it.

The flooring is of stone. There are thirty-seven steps leading up to the roof. There is no grave inside and the spot is famous as the 'Masjid ka Darwaza'. Basheeruddin Ahmad, however said that it has been built like a regular *gumbad* and does not seem to be a 'Masjid ka Darwaza'. He feels that it is a regular tomb to which this mosque is attached, as in the case of Isa Khan's tomb and mosque.

The dome is an extremely fine one; the walls of the building are not buttressed, as one might have expected in a building erected at the beginning of the sixteenth century. The exterior of the doorways is decorated with black and red stone after the fashion of the time, afterwards adopted for the gateway of the Purana Qila. The interior is dark, stern and impressive; the pendentives, although similar to those of the Alai Darwaza, are formed as true arches and niches above give the dome its height. Lastly, the heavy lintels and brackets, some of which are very fine, show the influence of the earlier Hindu style.

The mosque is of massive masonry, with the buttresses and sloping corner-towers characteristic of earlier times. The plaster decoration on the arches, and inside, is picked out with paint. An inscription announces the building of the mosque in the time of Sikandar Lodi, around 1500 AD.

The mosque measures 87 feet by 21 feet. There are two columns behind it for support, peeping over the roof. These also have four small openings inside them. The central mihrab of the masjid is 25 feet by 19 feet with a 2 feet *kangura*. The adjoining mihrabs are 16 feet wide and the mihrabs on the corners are 9 feet wide. There is an eave surrounding these mihrabs.

According to Basheeruddin Ahmad, there used to be a 110 feet by 87 feet platform in front of the mosque, the remnants of which we can see. There are some graves inside.

To the east, there is a three-arched hallway with two windows on the corners. It measures 55 feet by 12 feet. The height is 19 feet and there is a twelve-step staircase to go the top. This was probably a madrasa attached to the mosque.

Sheesh Gumbad

Sheesh Gumbad

Built by a Lodi chief, this *gumbad* is made of Kashani tiles. There are eight graves inside, plastered with cement by the British Government this is why we have no idea who the persons buried within are. There is a central entrance towards the south with azure blue tiles. Basheeruddin Ahmad said there were originally ninety-eight tiles.

Sultan Sikandar Lodi's Tomb

Huzuur e yaar huyi daftar e junuun ki talab
Girah mein le ke gireba'n ka taar taar chale
The beloved has summoned me to her court with my documents of infatuation
I have only my torn to tatters collar, which I take tied in a knot
Faiz Ahmed Faiz

Sikandar Lodi died in Agra on 21 November 1517 AD. His son, Ibrahim Shah Lodi, brought his body from there and buried him in this tomb built by him.

Sultan Sikander Lodi's tomb

Since the seventy-five-year Lodi reign saw more fighting than consolidation, the architecture of this period is more austere than that of the Mughals who succeeded them.

The most important structural feature of the tomb is the double dome, which was designed to preserve the symmetry and relative proportions of the body of the building. This feature was probably borrowed from Iran. The first double dome can be found in the tomb of Shihabuddin Taj Khan (1501 AD), locally called Bagh e Alam Ka Gumbad. This was later extensively copied by the Mughals and helped in the innovation of their style. This *gumbad* is inside a walled enclosure with battlements measuring 264 square feet, which had *burjis* or towers on all four sides out of which two remain.

The main gateway of the tomb is on the south wall and is 5 feet 19 inches wide. In the front is a platform at the height of 20 feet with nine steps leading up to it. These are extremely worn out and one has to walk carefully as there's a danger of slipping if not paying full attention.

The tomb is 55 square feet and has two *burjis* standing on four columns on either side. They were ornamented with coloured tiles, of which only a few remain. There is a mosque set in the west wall of the compound, with a central arch of 65 feet × 39 feet and smaller ones on the side.

It is an elegantly built tomb of lime and mortar with one grave inside it. There are sixteen niches out of which four are open for ventilation, ornamented with few remaining tiles. On the top circle of the ceiling, *ayat ul kursi* has been inscribed in red.

The surrounding galleries of the tomb are 9 feet wide. The ceiling and the doorway arches are very pretty, despite the fact that most of the tiles have fallen down. There was a staircase to go up to the dome but it is now closed. It still gives the impression of past grandeur.

The octagonal design and galleries of this tomb are similar to the tomb of Sultan Muhammad Shah close by. The difference is only in the size and the fact that Sultan Sikandar Lodi's tomb is inside a compound within a deep sloping hollow. Near it is a bridge of seven piers, which spans a water channel and is known as Athpula. This must have been the original approach to the gardens of Sultan Sikandar Lodi.

According to Basheeruddin Ahmad, there used to be an ancient and big *baoli* inside an enclosure with a grand darwaza, which was famous as Bagheechi.

Monuments inside Delhi Golf Club

The Delhi Golf Club is a municipal course established in the early 1930s. It became a corporate entity on 24 February 1950. Situated on erstwhile Mughal lands known as Babarpur, it was built around monuments.

I knew that there were three important tombs inside the Delhi Golf Club but nothing prepared me for the veritable feast that it is for a historian like me. The Delhi Golf Club hosted me with great courtesy and I was given a tour of the grounds on a golf cart when I visited. There is a wealth of funerary heritage inside its grounds, a reminder of why Delhi is known as a necropolis.

The verdant greens of the Golf Club were a soothing sight for sore eyes in the heat of May.

Lal Bangla

Lal Bangla

> *Tuk hirs-o-hawas ki chhod miyan, mat des bides phire mara,*
> *Qazzaaq ajal ka loote hai din raat, baja kar naqqara*
> *Wander not looking for worldly wealth; abandon the greed and avarice in man,*
> *The pirate of death is on the prowl to loot your days and night with the beat of a drum*
>
> *Nazeer Akbarabadi*

These are a set of tombs built for a royal family, now acting as a background to the new ruling class while they play golf.

In *Asar-us-Sanadid*, Sir Syed wrote that someone from the harem of Nasiruddin Mohammad Humayun Badshah was buried here. Badshah Shah Alam II later buried his mother, Lal Kunwar, in a small domed building in the same place.

There is much confusion around the identitiy of Lal Kunwar. This is not Lal Kunwar, the beloved of Jahandar Shah, but the mother of Shah Alam II, who shared the same name.

Shah Alam II built a mausoleum in 1779 AD. There are two domed monuments here. According to Sir Syed, Lal Kunwar's grave is in the building with the smaller dome and Begum Jaan, the daughter of Shah Alam II, is buried in the building with the bigger dome; but I found two graves in the smaller monument and none in the larger one. It is possible that the second grave in the smaller monument belonged to a relative of the royal family, which is not surprising since many cenotaphs have disappeared over the years. The bigger dome also housed the graves of Mirza Sultan Parvez and Mirza Dara Bakht, the brother of the heir apparent, Mirza Daood. The wives of the emperor are also buried here.

Both domes are similar in design, with square corner rooms, oblong halls between them and a square room in the centre. I climbed up to the top of both the mausoleums. The dome of the smaller one looked disproportionately large up close but is in very good condition. The pinnacles are still intact. The larger mausoleum also has a smaller dome. From these structures, one can get a good view of the Golf Club.

The buildings here are made completely of red sandstone and this, coupled with the name of Lal Kunwar, leads to the popular name Lal Bangla.

Some of the decorative motifs on its walls are still visible and testify to its original beauty.

Many scions of the Mughals were buried here. We know that Bahadur Shah II had an enclosure built in the courtyard with the grave of Nawab Fatehabadi Begum and another of Mirza Bulaqi. No traces of these graves remain now.

A separate compound of these monuments is maintaind by the ASI and can be accessed from the Delhi Golf Club parking lot.

Tomb of Saiyyed Abid

Tomb of Saiyyed Abid

Maut ka ek din mu'ayya'n hai
Neend kyun raat bhar nahin aati
When the day of death is fixed
Why is it so difficult to sleep?

Mirza Ghalib

Nawab Khan Dauran e Khan built the tomb for Saiyyed Abid Khan when he died in battle. It was also known as Shaheed ki Dargah.

This tomb was probably built in 1626 AD and is located near Lal Bangla inside the Golf Club premises. It is built of lime mortar and bricks, with glazed tiles for decoration.

There is confusion between the accounts of Sir Syed and Maulvi Zafar Hasan about this tomb.

Sir Syed's account goes as follows: 'This is an attractive building with a grand darwaza and pretty *sehdari* (three-door pavilion). The *burj* is also very elegant. It had an attractive tank and water channels in the courtyard but these are now desolate. All of it is in a ruinous state and the tile work has disappeared. Though it is no longer in a pristine condition, it's a reminder of grand old days.'

According to Maulvi Zafar Hasan, 'The tomb consists of a room 14 feet 3 inches square inside, its outer plan being octagonal in form.' He claims this has led to another standalone tomb nearby that has come to be known as Saiyyed Abid's tomb. He does not mention the gateway or water channel and this may have added to the confusion, leading the ASI to name the standalone tomb.

Sir Syed has also made a sketch of the tomb in front of the swimming pool area as the tomb of Syed Abid. I would rather believe him.

The calligraphic inscriptions that were part of this monument have been plastered over now. Remnants are visible on some tiles of its facade. I did not get a chance to see if there was a grave inside.

As the tomb labelled Saiyyed Abid Khan's tomb is not his, it is probably that of Mir Taqi, a Mughal about whom we know little. Both monuments were built with Lakhauri brick masonry, a brick dome and stone floors.

Vaulted Tomb

Just down the dirt track on my tour of the Golf club, I saw a vaulted tomb built on a raised platform. The oblong chamber measures 19 feet 9 inches by 11 feet 7 inches square, with three arched entrances on the longer side and two on the shorter side. This is probably a tomb from the Mughal era, built in Lakhauri brick masonry, though there are no graves visible. The tomb is shaped differently from the others in the vicinity.

Ruins of a Masjid

There are the remains of a plinth in the dense undergrowth, which could be a mosque mentioned by Maulvi Zafar Hasan. He speaks of a 40 feet by 34 feet square mosque on a raised platform comprising a courtyard and a western wall furnished with three mihrabs in this area. At the time of his writing (in 1919), only the central mihrab was extant and the courtyard had unknown graves overgrown with vegetation. A piece of wall stood forlorn and graves all along the path gave it an eerie feel.

Barah Khamba

Nothing prepared me for the beauty that confronted my eyes as I approached Hole No. 17 of the golf grounds. It is one of the prettiest tombs I have ever seen. Dating back to the Lodi era, it is in the form of a cross. Though only ten pillars remain of the original twelve (which give it its name), it is magnificent.

Four other smaller domed compartments surround the central dome (the eastern one has fallen). The tomb has been buttressed recently to support the pillars on the north and south. Though there are no signs of any ornamentation, its striking design did not need any.

The tomb, built of stone, contains one solitary grave. The person buried was probably a noble.

Barah Khamba

Early Mughal Tomb

Early Mughal Tomb

We soon came upon another square tomb, octagonal from the outside and square inside, with three unknown graves in a ruinous condition inside. It is a domed tomb with arched entrances on all four sides. Over each of these entrances are two arched openings, one above the other, admitting light.

The walls and ceilings have painted designs that are faded but attractive. Traces of colour and incised patterns can be seen on the arched doorways. The dome is built of brick.

Baghichi (Small Garden)

This was a garden enclosed by four walls, with a low arched doorway as entrance. The entrance has long since disappeared and the garden is now a part of the wilderness that surrounds it. The compound wall of the club runs alongside this garden.

The dome is surrounded by *chhatris*, two of which still remain. There is delicate stucco work on the exterior. It is built of Lakhauri bricks from the late Mughal period. Each square side has a recessed arch with a flat doorway. There are two unknown graves within.

During the Commonwealth Games of 2010, many monuments in the city got a makeover and this one did too. It now has a pretty ceiling with a striking floral design in incised plaster.

There are remnants of 'guldaan' (flower vases), incised in the plaster over the arched doorways. When newly built, they must have looked magnificent.

Stone was used for the flooring and Lakhauri brick masonry for the walls. The dome is also built of brick.

Mughal Masjid

Across from this erstwhile garden, on an another putting green, was what looked like a mosque. A trip closer revealed it to be a mosque from the Mughal period, standing on a *chabutra*.

Only two of the three original domed compartments built of brick masonry now remain. The arches of the remaining two are in poor condition. There is a courtyard in front of these.

Unknown Tomb

The Golf Club still hid some secrets and a short ride in the golf cart led us to a closely guarded one.

There were glimpses of a brown hue in the undergrowth at a distance. On walking into a path with thorns and brambles, I found a tomb in ruins with its Lakhauri bricks showing.

Maulvi Zafar Hasan mentions a few more tombs in terrible condition in the vicinity. The many changes this area has seen has probably left them in dust and ashes.

XI

RK Puram Tombs

Wazirpur Tombs

Teen Burji, Mohammadpur

Surag umr e guzishta ka dhoondiye gar Zauq
Tamam umr guzar jaaye justujoo karte
If one were to look for clues of life gone by, Zauq
Our whole lives would be spent in that quest

Sheikh Ibrahim Zauq

Since we have Wazir Khan of Wazirpur fame and Munir Khan of Munirka fame, it is my personal opinion that this village was named after a Mohammad Khan who built it. It could be from the Lodi period (1451–1526 AD). It

Mohammadpur Burj

measures 162 feet by 60 feet with three huge arched doors measuring 29 feet wide. Two of the doors have now been blocked and just have small windows; the main door has a grill and is opened by the ASI personnel on duty. It is built of large blocks of stone, once finished with plaster. Today, however, the plaster has disappeared.

Two heavy octagonal bastions flank the tomb. It is heavily encroached on three sides. In the front is a narrow road leading to the village. There is a huge central dome and two flatter domes. On the western wall is the mihrab which may once have had calligraphic decorations. One can see bits and pieces of calligraphic inscriptions around the drum of the central dome.

This monument actually looks like a mosque from afar. It is possible that it was used for burial when it fell into disuse. There are three compartments inside with innumerous unknown graves. Burial inside sacred spaces such as mosques and dargahs of saints is considered auspicious for the departed soul.

There are no inscriptions in the monument to give any clue of its origin or purpose. The roof of both the side compartments has a beautiful floral design seen in Sultan Muhammad Shah's tomb in Lodi Park. Though blackened by soot and time, it is haunting in its beauty. Like so many monuments in Delhi, it was used as a place of shelter and a cattle shed in the early twentieth century, only evacuated in the 1920s.

Masjid and Tomb of Haji Langa

Zindagi tu ne lahoo leke diya kuchh bhi nahin!
Tere daaman mein kya mere liye? kuchh bhi nahin!
O Life! What have you given me in return for my blood?
Is there nothing in your lap for me?

Rajesh Reddy

Tomb of Haji Langa

This is a monument in Sector 3 of RK Puram, built in the erstwhile district of Zamarudpur during the reign of Sultan Sikandar Lodi in around 1494 AD.

Near it is a lovely and high *gumti*, or a small building with a *kharbooza*, a fluted dome. This was, in all probability, a tomb but is today occupied by a gentleman who was most reluctant to let me enter. I managed to persuade him and saw his meagre possessions hanging on the wall, along with a small cot. The monument is well-maintained by the madrasa committee from the outside. Inside, it is ravaged, with black exposed stones and gaping holes.

There is a single bay and a three-arched ancient mosque that has been converted into a madrasa, now called Taleem ul-Quran. In 1992, Maulana Mohammad Qasim Rahimi and a few men started five-time prayers in the mosque, laying the foundation of a madrasa. The madrasa is a multi-storeyed building and hides the white dome of the tomb, which used to be visible from the Outer Ring Road.

Bijri Khan ka Gumbad

Hayaat-o-maut do kadiyaa'n hai ik zanjeer ki Afsar
Koi kya ibtida samjhe, koi kya intiha jaane
Life and death are two links of the same chain Afsar
No one can understand its origin or end

Afsar Merathi

Constructed of rubble masonry, this is a massive building measuring 59 square feet. The dome springs from a sixteen-sided drum and is crowned with a red sandstone and marble pinnacle. It is on a higher level than the road and can be seen very clearly by all passers-by.

It is similar to Bare Khan ka Gumbad and other Lodi-era tombs, with its walls relieved with arched panels and an arch in the centre in which a

Bijri Khan ka Gumbad

doorway is set on three sides. The western wall does not have a door but instead the mihrab for the *qiblagah*.

There are stairs leading to the top via the eastern door. Though there is little space around the dome, we got a magnificent view of the surrounding area when we went up. It contains four graves.

INTACH has marked the tomb of Bijri Khan as Grade 'A' under the archaeological rating system, which makes the structure a significant archaeological site (more significant than ancient and protected historical sites). This tomb was said to be in quite a bad state and was repaired before the Commonwealth Games of 2010.

Next to the main tomb is a smaller *gumbad* with an unknown grave. Prior to 1924, these tombs were in the possession of villagers and used as fodder store. This is also in Sector 3, RK Puram, next to a slum.

Munda Gumbad

Maut agarche maut hai
Maut se ziist kam nahin
If death is final
Life too is fatal

Firaq Gorakhpuri

This *gumbad* is distinct with a cylindrical neck but no dome. It is this dome-less feature that gives it its name: Munda (bald).

It is constructed of rubble and measures 34 square feet. Each of the four sides of the building is pierced by an arched doorway giving access into the chamber inside.

In the side walls are staircases leading to the roof, on which there are grey stone bases of pillars belonging to an upper storey that no longer exists.

Munda Gumbad

There are two possibilities for the lack of a dome, since the provision for it has been made. One, that it was architecturally weak and fell down; or two, that it could not be completed.

There is a single grave inside it and, with the open sky above, it looks peaceful. The *gumbad* is well worth a visit, offering solitude and repose, and is situated in a residential colony opposite a government school in Sector 4, RK Puram.

Wazirpur Tombs

Nazar fareb e kaza khaa gayi to kya hoga
Hayaat maut se takra gayi to kya hoga
What if one is blinded by the illusion of death?
What if life collides with death?

Ehsaan Danish

Wazirpur Tombs

A very popular park, this area provides solace and greenery to many living in tiny flats and cramped quarters in and around Delhi. The pursuit of life amidst tombstones is a very common sight in the city.

The Wazirpur tombs are a group of five tombs of unknown Lodi nobles, believed to have taken their names from the area they were built in. However, Basheeruddin Ahmad mentions a man called Wazir Khan who was buried here. It is possible this may have been his jageer and the area was named after him.

The first tomb is 20 square feet and is small enough to be referred to as 'gumzi' in nineteenth-century texts. The second tomb is the largest and grandest; it is the tomb of Wazir Khan, measuring 60 square feet. This rubble masonry structure, originally plastered, has triple-arched openings on three sides. The mihrab recess occupies the central archway on the western side. Under the dome is a stone grave. It belongs to the Lodi period. The third and fourth tombs are very similar, each measuring 26 square feet. In the fourth tomb, there is a rubble grave.

In front of the second tomb is a fifth tomb, which is 15.5 square feet in area, and a small domed building, which has been converted into a storage area and is kept locked. It was probably made at a later date than the other four.

As with the rest of Delhi, the locals venerate the person buried here and the central tomb has offerings of oil, jaggery, garlands and flowers in it, adding to the charm of the place.

There have been reports of people living inside these monuments, though I personally did not find any traces of people when I visited.

Its expansive and well-maintained lawns and trees make it a popular place for people to sit and hang out. It is an oasis of calm in a busy city.

South of the tombs is a simple two-tier *baoli*. Two pavilions flank the *baoli* with the well in between, which is totally dry now. Interestingly, this is the first *baoli* I have seen which has water channels running out of it. This seems to suggest that the area may have been under cultivation since household and personal needs would have been met within the *baoli* itself.

There is a wall mosque near the *baoli*. It is on a raised platform with a five-recessed mihrab wall on the west. There is a grave in the centre of the platform, which gives rise to the theory that the mosque was built to serve as prayer niche for it. In my opinion, the grave could not have come up later; that would require digging up the mosque platform and building the cenotaph on top. The mosque is in Sector 5, RK Puram.

Bada Lao ka Gumbad

Zafar aadmi uss ko na jaaniyega, vo ho kaisa hi saheb e fahm-o-zaka
Jisse aish mein yaad e Khuda na rahi, jisse taish mein
khauf e Khuda na raha
Zafar doesn't count human a man, be he a man of understanding
and charity
If he doesn't remember God in moments of happiness, or doesn't
fear God when angry.

Bahadur Shah Zafar

Bada Lao ka gumbad

This Lodi-era tomb is situated in a park in Basant Lok and is very popular with morning walkers and fitness enthusiasts. The tomb itself is kept locked and can be opened on request. It is quite a big one with an enclosing wall and circular bastions on its corners.

One has to climb up a few steps to reach up to the level. It is a square domed tomb with three arched doorways and a mihrab in the west. The ceiling of the dome is very beautiful with incised, painted decorations and has been recently restored.

A family had been living inside it for three generations since 1948 but they were evicted when preparations were being made for the Commonwealth Games in 2010. They had painted it pink from inside and had added electrical fittings and water supply to it.

There were four unknown graves in it that were destroyed at some point, probably by the encroachers. At the side of the tomb is a wall mosque, as these were found near tombs for the caretakers of the tomb and well wishers of the deceased to pray in.

An enclosed empty space is adjacent to the tomb, divided by the stairs. It is not clear what its purpose could have been but it is obviously a part of the complex.

Moradabad ki Pahari

Charha mansoor sooli par, jo wakif tha wohi dilbar
Arey mullah janaza parh, mein jaanoon mera khuda jaaney
Mansoor was hanged, only those who knew his love for God
understood his total annihilation of himself in God's love
O priests recite his funeral prayers, it's between me and my God
Hazrat Shah Niaz

Inside the Aravali forest is a spectacularly renovated group of mosques and tombs from the Lodi and Tughlaq era. Keeping Maulvi Zafar Hasan as a reference guide, Qasim and I had set off to find the mosque complex in the area known as Moradabad ki Pahari. We came upon a fancy gate and compound wall. Upon requesting, we were allowed inside.

During the Tughlaq era, a saint by the name of Syed Murad Ali Baba Shah settled in the Aravali forest. This area got named Moradabad Ki Pahari after him. It has nothing to do with the city Moradabad, which is named after Prince Murad Baksh, son of Emperor Shah Jahan.

His tomb is old and survives in its ruinous original state but his grave seems to have been renovated. The date of his death is given as 732 Hijri or

Moradabad ki Pahadi

1331 AD. The tomb is inside the madrasa compound and he is still revered by people of all faiths; locals come here often to offer flowers and prayers.

Whether the madrasa and *khanqah* developed around it, or if it was already present in his lifetime, is not clear. My guess would be that the first building was after his passing away during the period of Sultan Firoz Shah Tughlaq, as the solid architecture seems to date back to it.

There are two distinct buildings, with the one on the left being Tughlaq and the one on the right Lodi as it has a lotus *kalash* which was developed under the Lodis and was being built in domes.

It's called Qasai ka Gumbad and Shahi Masjid. They have both been restored and are in an excellent state of preservation.

The madrasa is called the Abdul Mannan Academy. According to Maulvi Rashid, the imam here, his father Maulana Abdul Mannan, got the papers searched for it and established a madrasa forty years ago. It is he who got it restored as he was fond of heritage preservation.

Friday congregational prayers are held here and it is popular with the embassy staff of Islamic countries, who have their offices in Vasant Vihar.

XII

Central Delhi Dargahs

Bhuli Bhatiyari ka Mahal

Dargah Hazrat Rasool Numa

I travelled a long way seeking God,
but when I finally gave up and turned back,
there He was, within me!
O Lalli!
Now why do you wander
like a beggar?
Make some effort,
and He will grant you
a vision of Himself
in the form of bliss
in your heart.

Lalla Ded[64]

Dargah Hazrat Rasool Numa

This Dargah is on Qutub Road and was designed by an engineer, so it is different from other dargahs in style. The shrine is open to the air. Hazrat Rasool Numa was a very famous saint during the reign of Aurangzeb. He received the title of Rasool Numa (revealer of the Prophet) because he had reached such a degree of closeness to the Prophet (pbuh) on account of his devotions that he would reveal the Prophet to his disciples on the very first night of their becoming his disciple. He died in 1691 AD.

Dargah Hazrat Khuda Numa

Die to yourself – no longer stay apart,
But give to Him who asks for it your heart;
The man whose happiness derives from Him
Escapes existence, and the world grows dim;
Rejoice for ever in the Friend, rejoice
Till you are nothing, but a praising voice.

Fariduddin Attar[65]

A little way towards the west of Hazrat Rasool Numa is the dargah of Hazrat Khuda Numa. He was a saint in the era of Aurangzeb.

Bhuli Bhatiyari ka Mahal

Khud pukaregi jo manzil to thahar jaaunga
Warna khuddar musafir hu'n guzar jaaunga
If the destination itself calls me, I will stop
Else, I'm a self-respecting person, I will pass it by

Muzaffar Razmi

This is a famous area in the central ridge reserve forest. They are the ruins of a palace built by Bu Ali Bakhtiyari in 1354 AD, during the reign of Sultan Firoz Shah. This has been distorted to Bhuli Bhatiyari ka Mahal.

Bhuli Bhatiyari ka Mahal

It was built on a hilltop and had a wonderful view from the top. During monsoons, it used to be popular resort.

There was a well-made dam built by Sultan Firoz Shah at this place. Sir Syed was of the opinion that the dam and palace were both built by Sultan Firoz Shah.

In the month of Asadh (June–July) on the night of the full moon, a fair was held here called Pavan Parichha (wind testing). In this fair the Brahmins would put their flagstaff in the ground and could predict the weather from that. A huge gathering of Hindus and Muslims would participate. Today it lies in wilderness and is said to be haunted because of the wilderness around it.

Anand Vivek Taneja speculates that the nearby Jhandewalan Mandir may have been named because of the flags that were planted in this hunting lodge by the Brahmins to test the flow of the wind and predict the weather for the year.

XIII

Historical Trails

Dargah Hazrat Yusuf Qattal (Courtesy: ASI archives)

1. Siri Walk – 1

Keep walking on the road that goes into the Siri Fort Sports Complex until you reach the Siri Fort Children's Museum. Here you will find:

- Some parts of the Siri Fort Walls and Mohammad Wali mosque. Nili Masjid is a short walk from here in Kharera village. From here, walk to the residential colony of Hauz Khas.
- Dargah Makhdoom Sabzwari – inside Mayfair Gardens
- Chor Minar and Eidgah – inside R Block, Hauz Khas on opposite side of Mayfair Gardens
- On the road leading to Hauz Khas village from Aurobindo Marg, you can see The Walls of Kharera – it is private property so you can only see it from the Aurobindo Marg.

2. Siri Walk – 2

As you walk towards Hauz Khas village, you will find these tombs on either side of the road:

- Dadi Poti ka Mazar, Biran ka Gumbad, Choti Gumti, Sakri Gumti, Barah Khamba
- Before you reach the Hauz Khas village you will see a sign saying *Deer Park on your right*. Enter that to see: Bagh e Alam ka Gumbad, Kali Gumti and Tuhfewala Gumbad
- Come out, walk towards the village and enter the Hauz Alai/Hauz Khas monument complex. You will find: Hauz Alai, Sultan Firoz Shah Madrasa, Sultan Firoz Shah Tomb and the reservoir, Hauz Alai.

3. Siri Walk – 3

- Go into Shahpur Village and see the remnants of the Siri Wall fortifications, Tuhfewala Gumbad. The entrance to this is from inside the lanes.
- Walk into the 26-acre park that also houses remnants of Siri walls and a lovely bridge. This is quite an enjoyable walk.
- Opposite it, in the Asiad Village Complex, is the Bulbuliki mosque. It can be accessed from the park.

4. The Khirki Walk

- Start with a visit to the Khirki mosque opposite Select Citywalk Mall.
- From there, walk over to Satpula Dam and on to Khirki Village. On the road opposite Sadhana Enclave is the exquisite tomb of Hazrat Yusuf Qattal.
- From here, if you walk towards Sadhana Enclave, you can find the Lal Gumbad of Sheikh Kabiruddin Auliya.

5. The Chiragh-e-Dilli Walk

- The Chiragh-e-Dilli dargah complex can be accessed from Press Enclave Road in South Delhi.
- Walk around the village as you go to its entrance and you will find many old monuments which have been swallowed into residential colonies. The old gateways give away the tombs hiding inside the colonies.
- Once you have spent some time sitting in the tranquil environs of the dargah, you can visit the tomb of Bahlol Lodi.

6. Tughlaqabad and Adilabad Walk

This is quite a strenuous walk, so put on your walking shoes. Adilabad is on the same side of the road as the tomb.

7. The Surajkund Walk

This is best visited during the Surajkund Mela in February–March, when there's a lot more to explore.

8. The South Ex Walk

- One can start from Kale Khan ka Gumbad, which is in South Extension 1 behind the market. You can go inside the lane next to the Nalli Silks showroom. Just near it is the three-tomb complex of Bade Khan, Chote Khan and Bhure Khan. They are inside a park; you can ask locals for directions.
- Darya Khan's tomb is a short walk from here, across a small bridge near the Kidwai Nagar post office. The area is known as Dr Shyama Prasad Mukerjee Chowk.
- From here, the walk through Mubarakpur Kotla village is a slightly longer one. It is difficult to reach without asking for directions from locals. Ask for the *gumbad*. Climb on to one of the many buildings there to appreciate its beauty as it's completely surrounded by them. You can wander inside after that. Once there you can ask for directions to the mosque, which is through the houses.

9. The Begumpur Walk

- Start with Bijay Mandal opposite Sarvapriya Club in Hauz Khas (behind Laxman School metro station stop).
- Go on to Begumpur Masjid and then Sarai Shahji, which is in the village. You can ask for directions. The tomb of Farid Khan Bukhari is near Sarai Shahji.

10. The Firoz Shah Kotla Walk

- A good time to visit is after 2 p.m. on Thursdays. You will see people offering flowers and incense sticks to the jinns that are believed to reside in the premises. The place is full of people, mostly from Old Delhi. They come there to offer prayers, have fun or celebrate the fulfilment of their wishes by distributing biryani in huge pots. If you don't like the crowds, it's advisable to visit on any other day.

- Khooni Darwaza is at the entrance to the fort. The Dargah of Hazrat Badruddin Samarqandi can be accessed from the opposite side. It is in the Rose Garden, Balmiki Basti in Vikram Nagar, off NH-44.

11. The Paharganj Walk

- One can enter Paharganj and go on to Qutub Road, Singara Chowk. From here you can ask the way to Qila Qadam Sharif or just Qila, as it's known in Nabi Karim, and walk into the winding alleys till you reach it.
- On the way, you will pass many old and dilapidated structures. There are still remnants of the gateways of the Qila. On your way back, ask around for the route to Ustad Zauq's memorial. It is in the one of the alleys near the rubbish dump.

12. The Poet's Walk

- Near Maulana Azad Medical College, you can ask for Mehndiya'n and walk into the cemetery to find the graves of Shah Waliullah and the poet Momin Khan Momin.
- From here, you can walk towards Zakir Husain College. Near it is a lane called Mir Dard (next to a petrol pump). Walk inside till you reach a green tin structure, which houses the remains of the famous mystic poet.

13. The Sultan Raziya Walk

- Start from Turkman Gate and walk till Mohalla Qabristan to visit the shrine of Shah Turkman Bayabani.
- Go to Kalan Masjid and, from there, to Bulbulikhana. A signboard there on a residential colony will direct you to Sultan Raziya's grave.

14. The Zamarudpur Walk

- Enter the Zamarudpur area from the lane near Bluebells School.
- Once you're there, ask for directions for the *gumbads*. It's not a very friendly place for tourists who want to see the encroached tombs.

15. The RK Puram Walk

- One can start with the Teen Burj inside Mohammadpur village, near Bikaji Cama Place.
- From here, you can drive (a walk advisable only in good weather) to Sector 3, RK Puram and find Bijri Khan's tomb off the main road.
- You can proceed to the lanes of Sector 5, RK Puram, opposite the Kendriya Vidyalaya School and see the Munda Gumbad.
- You can end the walk at the Wazirpur tombs, which are also in Sector 5. It could be done in reverse but I feel concluding an exploratory walk in a park instead of a crowded lane is a better experience.
- The Haji Langa tomb complex is on the Ring Road in RK Puram. However, since it's a functioning madrasa, tourists and visitors are not encouraged.

Notes and References

1. Catherine Asher, *The New Cambridge History of India*, Cambridge University Press, 1992.
2. Journal II, Archeological Survey of India.
3. Hazrat Amir Khusrau, *Khazainul Futuh*, trans. Mohammad Habib, (Madras: Diocesan Press).
4. Hereafter referred to as Sir Syed.
5. M.M. Kaye, ed., *The Golden Calm*, Webb & Bower, 1980.
6. From Basheeruddin Ahmad's book *Waqiat-e-Darul-Hukumat.*
7. Originally written in Turkish. English translation by Murat Yagan.
8. Mohammad Habib, *Hazrat Amir Khusrau of Delhi* (New Delhi: Cosmo Publications, 2006).
9. A Prophet who is said to have discovered the fountain of life and drunk it, guide, leader. This story is quoted by Basheeruddin Ahmad.
10. Iḥyā' Ulūm al-Dīn 2/278.
11. General Alexander Cunningham was the founder and first director general of Archaeological Survey of India in 1861.
12. Report for the Year 1871-72, Archaeological Survey of India.
13. Mohammad Habib, *Hazrat Amir Khusrau of Delhi* (New Delhi: Cosmo Publications, 2006).
14. This is, as the name suggests, a building with twelve doors designed to allow free flow of air.
15. Translation by Rohini Bakshi.

16. Translation by Acharya Ramanuja Devanathan.
17. Translated from the Persian by Afkham Darbandi and Dick Davis.
18. Vidushi Sagar, 'The dargah at the IGI Airport', *Deccan Herald,* June 23, 2015, New Delhi.
19. Yahya-bin-Ahmad-bin-Abdullah Sirhindi, *Tarikh e Mubarakshahi*, trans. Henry Beveridge.
20. Ibid.
21. Carr Stephen, *The Archaeology and Monumental Remains of Delhi* (New Delhi: Aryan Books International, 2002).
22. Verse from Basheeruddin Ahmad, *Waqiat-e-Darul-Hukumat Dehli*, translation by Usman Ghani and Rana Safvi.
23. Gordon Risley Hearn, *The Seven Cities of Delhi*, (New Delhi: Adarsh Press, 2013).
24. *Manilkara hexandra* – a small- to medium-sized evergreen tree.
25. Translated from the original in Punjabi by Paul Smith.
26. Translated from original in Kashmiri by *Dr Krishna Raina.*
27. Quoted by Basheeruddin Ahmad.
28. Tim Mackintosh-Smith, 'A Tangerine in Delhi', *Aramco World*, March/April 2006, p. 14-23.
29. Sir Alexander Cunningham (23 January 1814–28 November 1893) was a British army engineer with Bengal Engineer Group whose interest in Indian archaeology and history saw him appointed as the first archaeological surveyor to the government of India in 1861. He founded and organized what later became the Archaeological Survey of India.
30. J.D. Beglar was Cunningham's assistant and instrumental in documenting much of India's archaeological heritage.
31. Carr Stephen, *The Archaeology and Monumental Remains of Delhi* (New Delhi: Aryan Books International, 2002).
32. Referenced from the story in the Quran when swallows protected the Kaaba from the forces of Abraha.
33. Shams Siraj Afif, *Tarikh-e-Firoz Shahi*, trans. Elliott & Dawson, (History of India as told by its own historians).

34. Carr Stephen, *The Archaeology and Monumental Remains of Delhi* (New Delhi: Aryan Books International, 2002).
35. Translated from original in Marathi by Mahatma Gandhi.
36. Translated from the original in Persian by Vraje Abramian.
37. Translated from original Persian by Jonathan Star and Shahram Shiva.
38. Translated from the original in Persian by David and Sabrineh Fideler.
39. This chronogram is written in the *ta'miya* style (which is a puzzle with inbuilt clues) in which for the correct date to be taken out, some letters from the rest of the verse have to be added to the chronogramical kernel, Zauq jannati, which gives the year 1269 AH whereas he died in 1271 AH. So the words 'sar e bakshish' is also a clue that the head of the word bakshish which is the 'b' whose numerical value is two, has to be added to get the correct year of death.
40. Translated from original Persian by Nasim Fekrat.
41. Ibid.
42. Maulavi Kabir Al-Din Ahmed, *The Muntakhab Al-Lubab of Khafi Khan.*
43. Dr Abdul Ghani, *Life and Works of Abdul Qadir Bedil.*
44. This is according to Sir Syed Ahmad Khan in *Asar-us-Sanadid.* Historian Catherine Asher, however, feels that it was 'almost certainly built' by Humayun and adds that 'Abu al-Fazl, the official chronicler of Humayun's son and successor, Akbar, writes that the building in which Humayun had his fatal accident had only recently been completed.' (*The New Cambridge History of India, Architecture of Mughal India*)
45. Ibid.
46. Translated from the original in Chinese by J.P. Seaton.
47. J.D. Beglar in a report for the Archaeological Survey of India.
48. *Sair-ul-Mutakharin, Asar-us-Sanadid, Tabqat-e-Akbari, Tarikh-i-Bada'uni, Tarikh-e-Ferishta.*
49. Translated from original in Tamil *by J.K. Mohana Rao.*
50. H.C. Fanshawe, *Delhi Past and Present* (New Delhi: Asian Educational Services, 1902).
51. Carr Stephen, *The Archaeology and Monumental Remains of Delhi* (New Delhi: Aryan Books International, 2002).

52. Verse from Basheeruddin Ahmad's *Waqiat-e-Darul-Hukumat Dehli.*
53. H.C. Fanshawe, *Delhi Past and Present* (New Delhi: Asian Educational Services, 1902).
54. Verse attributed to Khwaja Khizr. Mehru Jaffer, *The Book of Nizamuddin Auliya* (New Delhi: Penguin India, 2012).
55. There was a misprint in the text which read as '*mabdam kard*' but was corrected by Syed Faizan who said that the quartrain was not in correct metre as per the rules of a rubai.
56. Catherine Asher, *The New Cambridge History of India*, Cambridge University Press, 1992.
57. Abul Fazl, *Ain e Akbari*, trans. Blockmann & Jarret, Vol 1.
58. Khaliq Ahmed Nizami, *The Life and Times of Shaikh Nizamuddin Auliya* (New Delhi: Oxford University Press, 2007).
59. Basheerudin Ahmad, *Waqiat-e-Darul-Hukumat*, Dehli, Urdu Academy, New Delhi.
60. Khaliq Ahmed Nizami, *The Life and Times of Sheikh Nizamuddin Auliya* (New Delhi: Oxford University Press, 2007).
61. Amir Khurd, Siyar-ul-Auliya (Reference from Khaliq Ahmed Nizami).
62. Sangeet Natak, Volume XLII, No. 4, 2008.
63. H.C. Fanshawe, *Delhi Past and Present* (New Delhi: Asian Educational Services, 1902).
64. Translated by Swami Muktananda.
65. *Farid Attar, The Conference of Birds*, trans. Afkham Darbandi and Dick Davis, Penguin Classics, 1984.

Acknowledgements

A journey of a thousand steps starts by taking the first step out of the comfort zone. I thank Allah for giving me the strength to take that first step. I started my journey as a writer at the age of fifty-five and there have been many people who helped me along the way.

I'm thankful to Professor Catherine Asher, Ranjit Hoskote and Swapna Liddle for their generous praise for this book.

I am lucky I have Kanishka Gupta as my literary agent. He makes my life very easy. Not only does he pitch my work to publishers, he also encourages me to write more.

My partner in exploration, Syed Mohammad Qasim, not only complements my work with his sublime photography but is also a constant companion on my journeys in the city of Delhi. I learn so much from him. His tireless efforts at capturing the perfect image have made this book richer.

Syed Farid Nizami and Peerzada Altamash Nizami have made this book richer by not only sharing their inputs but also giving me great insights about the dargah of Hazrat Nizamuddin Auliya, as well as by ensuring I had access to many areas inaccessible to the general public.

The Archaeological Department of India has always been very generous and co-operative whenever I needed to study various monuments up close. I am particularly grateful to them for giving me access to rare and archival photographs of Delhi and for granting me permission to use them in my book.

I am blessed to receive affection and support from Professor Shamsur Rahman Faruqi, whose words of encouragement are always a source of inspiration. No matter what time of the day or night I message him, he unfailingly replies to my queries. (And believe me, I have many!)

I am fortunate to have met Ajmal Siddiqui, thanks to our shared love for Urdu poetry. He is always responsive to my calls and messages and has added incredible detailing to the translations of various verses used in this book. Not only did he translate many of them, he also explained the many nuances of language to me. May God give more power to his pen and bless him always.

Several of my friends contributed in translating the Urdu and Persian verses in this book. A huge shoutout to Usman Ghani from across the border in Pakistan and Dr Mohammad Taqi across the seven seas in Florida. I would often send them screenshots and they would respond via email or through Twitter's direct messages. The verses which may not read so well in translation are the ones I have attempted to translate myself. All mistakes, and I am sure there are many, are mine.

My family, especially my sisters, have always been there for me and Inshallah they always will. My love for them, always. I adore my lovely nieces and nephew, whose pride in me encourages me to achieve more. Subuhi and Baqar, you are my pride and strength: all my love for you, always. I love it that you think your Amma is 'cool'. May Allah bless you both. And thank you, Gazanfar, for being a pillar of support to me always.

The team at HarperCollins has always added value to my work, whether it is with the insightful edits by Arcopol Chaudhuri, brilliant artwork by Bonita Vaz-Shimray and Sanjeev Kumar, and beautiful typesetting and layout by Ashutosh Jha.

I would also like to acknowledge the many people who make my life easier so that I can write. One is Nagamani, who took care of our house while I was busy exploring Delhi. My driver, Atindra, drove me around without a complaint to every monument I was interested in visiting at any given hour of the day.

I'd particularly like to thank my readers for the love and support they continue to shower on me. Without them, I'm no one. I don't know if I deserve it but I do know, I will always cherish their interest in my writing that and work hard. Above all, I want to thank Maula Ali, Bibi Fatima, Qutub Sahab and Mehboob e Ilahi for their blessings and presence in my life and in books.